TWELVE-STEP WORKBOOK
13ᵗʰ STEP

A companion workbook series to Butterflies and Paratroopers Are Not Born with Wings:
A Warrior's Guide to BeingHappy, Joyous, and Free
Available on AMAZON.COM and at BPBOOKS.NET

MILO

\

Note To Reader

Beware! Those Raffle Ticket Romeo's are everywhere.

The 13th Step is not extra credit for doing the first twelve. And while you won't find them mentioned in the Big Book, those Raffle Ticket Romeo's are out there. With the information presented in this workbook you'll get the truth of what the 13th Step is, and be able to identify, prevent, and chase away any "thirteenth steppers" that come your way.

This workbook is one of the *Twelve Step Workbook* series by Milo Martin. But unlike the other workbooks, this one has no "check on learning" questions as part of the text. This is because there is no 13th step in the Big Book. Therefore, there are no directions. This means you can open this workbook anywhere and begin becoming a 13th Step subject matter expert. Not in doing, but in knowing.

The *13th Step Workbook* is a companion to the author's primary work, *Butterflies and Paratroopers Are Not Born With Wings: A Warrior Guide to Being Happy, Joyous, and Free.* In that book, Milo trains a butterfly to become a paratrooper. That's not easy. Neither is recovery from alcohol, drugs, food, people, or whatever. In that book, the persona of an Army First Sargent, trains the alcoholic to operate the most prone to breakdown, out of warranty, piece of equipment ever made. That's you.

In this book, the author shares his thirty-three years of observations and understanding of what thirteenth stepping is, and is not. Who are the perpetrators, and who is their prey. What can be done to identify, prevent, and hold account those who participate or those that ignore. While the subject of this workbook is no laughing matter, Milo with wit and sarcasm uses an iron fist in a velvet glove to educate and entertain.

The Twelve Steps are a design for living that seems to work for people like us. And who are the people like us? We are the ones that have tried everything else. Be you an alcoholic, drug addict, codependent, OCD, overeater, or whatever, these workbooks have the clear-cut simple directions millions have followed to understand what they are like, why they are like that, and why it's important to change.

As *Butterflies and Paratroopers,* and this series, relies heavily on the Big Book, reprint permission was sought and received from Alcoholics Anonymous World Services, Inc. Office of Intellectual Property before publication. While excerpts, in whole or part herein, are reprinted with permission of Alcoholics Anonymous World Services, Inc. it neither approves nor necessarily agrees with the views expressed. A.A. is a program of recovery for alcoholism only—use of the Twelve Steps in connection with programs and activities which are patterned after A.A., but which address other problems, or in any other non-A.A. context, does not imply otherwise.

Contents

Caveat Emptor

An *alcohonyism* is a made-up word. And like so many of our excuses, means nothing. There is no 13th step but there are thirteen "steppers". Nor is the 13th step extra credit for doing the first twelve.

A search of AAs literature and Webster's online yields no response for the 13th step. It is, however, an AA colloquial term whose meaning has changed over time. Per the informational site Quora Digest, once referred to someone who could drink in safety after completing the Twelve Steps. The same site also says it's a "jokey" way of referencing sex in the first year of recovery. The Urban Dictionary describes the 13th step, as the efforts of an old timer, to screw a newcomer. And that site refers to the adage, "Get'em before God does."

It's my belief that's it from that crude, but accurate assertion, the "thirteenth-stepper" who seeks sex with a newcomer gets their moniker. And what's meant by that saying? It's a maxim which for us means there is no middle-of-the-road solution. We have but two alternatives. One, go on to the bitter end, or two, pick up a kit of spiritual tools.

The thirteenth step is narrowly defined as when a newcomer is enticed, voluntarily or otherwise, into a sexual relationship with someone who has more sober time than they do. However, a wider application is àpropo. The broader definition is inclusive of when one sober alcoholic uses their sobriety status for personal, rather than principled goings-on. To illustrate. A red light once stopped me at a busy Boston intersection. One where a political candidate would post sign-holding supporters. Hearing a familiar voice yelling, "Hey Milo!" I thought I was at a meeting. There, holding signs reading Marty for Mayor, were a dozen AA members. Several Marty sponsored. I don't know if their presence was voluntary. If it wasn't by free choice, then they were being thirteenth stepped. For it its core, thirteenth stepping is when one alcoholic personally gains at the expense of another alcoholic.

A sponsor who gets a newcomer to wash their car, clean their house, lend them money, or any other non-recovery service is thirteenth stepping. "Volunteering" out of want of approval of a sponsor, newcomer or not, for promotion, influence peddling, campaigning, or ass kissing, qualifies too. This is because, stepping is taking advantage of a differential in perceived authority or superiority regarding recovery. Thirteenth stepping is supplanting God reliance with human reliance, hence the meaning of "Get'em before God does."

While we don't find the term 13th step in AA literature, nevertheless, it's part of the AA lingo. Most newcomers get acquainted with the term early in the recovery process. Regrettably, once they find out it's about sex, they can't wait to touch that hot stove.

Predatory behavior is not just about sex. Sometimes it's the means to material, emotional, and/or psychological wants and needs. Then again, sometimes it's just someone being mean. Thirteen-stepping in any form is wrong. It's not a victimless random occurrence. A successful thirteenth-stepper shows up at a meeting, knows the language, and who and what to look for. The thirteenth-stepper, hence "stepper" for short, is a crafty creature. Stealth, deception, and charisma, are their cover. They are part fox, part wolf, part jackal, and complete asshole. The prey the stepper leaves behind, like roadkill, remains for all to see. The most badly run-over always seem to want to go back for more.

The most popular game of chance is roulette. The second is the AA newcomer fling. In the first, we place a marker on the bet, in the second, we're the mark. Like with a one-night stand, office indiscretion, or internet video hook-up, with the 13th step, there's a sell-by date. You can only use one until it expires, and after that, it turns sour.

Nice to hear you. Wanna go for coffee? Need a ride? My wife just doesn't understand me. Can I read you the sex part of my fourth step? Can I sponsor you? You're so deep. Wanna see my Big Book? These are the thirteenth step calls of the wild. The prelude to the rehab romance and first meeting fling. After all, it's not like we're going drinking. Think again. It's the same thing, only different. So how then do we judge? Well to answer that, I'll refer to Supreme Court Justice Potter Stewart who said about obscenity, "I can't define it, but I know it when I see it." This means we can avoid it.

As strange as it seems, denial is a big part of the victimization process. "How can this happen? What did I do wrong? Is this my fault?" To which the stepper will answer, "Damn right it is." After all, in the stepper's way of thinking, it can't be their fault.

Avoiding isolation and taking part with the many is an AA inclusion thing. A stepper is like a sniper. They hide in plain sight, bide their time, observe the target, and take the shot. They pick off the ones who stray from the center of the herd. Steppers are sobriety killers.

It's those on the edge of AA who think they "got this" that are most at risk of being picked off. Once down, word gets around, and the jackals, hyenas, and wolves come to the feast one after another. Therefore, it's best to stay in the middle of the crowd under the watchful eye of those who will defend you until you can defend yourself.

And even if you are spiritually fit, off-ramp any idea that this time, or this one, will be different. That you can trust them because they say they are not like the others. When listening to yourself, if it sounds too good to be true, it probably isn't. There is nothing wrong with having hope, just don't bet your sobriety on it. In the stepper's worldview, the verdict of the ages is, that there's a sucker born every minute.

The addict's life is one of illusion and delusion. We tell ourselves the lie. That's the illusion. We believe the lie, that's the delusion. So, as you read along and suddenly a thought crosses your mind, "I've done that." This doesn't mean you're a closet stepper. For if you're reading this book, I doubt you're a psychopathic, predatory, serial stepper. Why? Because sunlight is the best disinfectant, and keeping hush-hush is the only way a stepper survives. The last thing a stepper wants to know about themselves, is the truth about themselves.

Also, human nature dictates that at some time, somewhere, and with someone, some thirteenth stepping behavior takes place in everyone's life. It's unavoidable. Why? Because we are not saints. So, if you have a reaction to what's written, it means nothing more than an honest self-appraisal is taking place. In swallowing and digesting some big chunks of truth about ourselves, we need not throw up all over ourselves.

The value of gold comes not from its rarity but from its permanence and purity. Dating in AA is not prohibited. Millions have found their life partner in the fellowship. This "boy meets girl on AA campus" story happens anywhere people mix and mingle. I'll wager for ninety-nine percent in AA, being pursued with pressure is not their experience. We watch out for each other and provide protection when warranted. I married an AA gal who wanted no part of me. I left her alone until all her friends told her, "You better take him. There is no one else left." The way I figure it, the only way I get into heaven is to say, "I'm with her."

Unlike the other books in the *Twelve Step Workbook* series, there are no clear-cut simple Big Book Step Study directions to be had. In this work, we acknowledge that while we may all be in the same boat, not everybody rows in the same direction. So, what we offer in these pages is some practical advice on how to identify, avoid, respond to, and recuperate from this infectious malady that threatens our fellowship. There are some rotten apples in our midst. These steppers come and go, but mostly they remain unseen. They get in and get out before they're found out. That's how they get away with it.

Does this mean that wherever two or more gather, there's a chance one will be bad? While unlikely, it's possible. Don't let this thought deter you. Instead, remember not to let your guard down and keep in mind. It's the sentry who's scared to death that keeps both eyes open.

We're not here to blame, shame, or accuse. Being in AA means we are on a life and death errand. And our primary purpose is to stay sober and help others recover from alcoholism. AA gives no guarantee that with sobriety, all will have no shortcomings. Keep in mind that if we are to recover, we cannot bury our skeletons or padlock the door. We grow by our willingness to face and rectify errors. In this work, we will try to maintain a sense of seriousness, sensibility, and responsibility.

Occasionally, an alcoholic is so damaged that we cannot help. They remain sick and deranged after putting down the drink. These are the ones who are constitutionally incapable of being honest with themselves. They suffer from grave emotional and mental disorders. Yet, no matter how deeply embedded these disorders may be, no one is so discredited or has sunk so low they should not be *welcomed*. All anyone asks for in coming into AA is another second chance, at another second chance.

But we will not sink the ship to save the man overboard. When we see someone sinking into the morass, muck, and mire of being a stepper, we have a responsibility to try and pull them out of the quicksand that surrounds them. For in seeing them slide under, we realize we too could be overcome by trials, tribulations, pandemonium, and predicaments. But then again, sometimes countless vain attempts yield no fruit. We make no excuses for bad behavior.

Outside the meeting hall, we keep few skeletons in the closet. The gossip grapevine is always ripe with rumors, innuendo, foibles, and fantasies. This does not differ from the non-alcoholic life. However, what we don't do is take advantage of, or have malicious intent toward each other. Instead, with a wink, a nod, and a smile, we laugh with, but never at each other. After all, if we didn't enjoy the sober way of living, we wouldn't pursue it. We think laughter, camaraderie, and good cheer sure beats trying to live life on life terms running on self-will run riot.

We are an assorted crowd. And while the subject in this book is no laughing matter, we aren't a glum lot. Our Rule 62 says that if this reading produces a sporadic giggle, that's okay. This give-and-take-tempered tongue-in-cheek sometimes gallows humor, let's us laugh at something that's not funny. That's alcoholism.

Sobriety is more than the inverse of inebriation. It's clarity of thought. We used to think one way, and now we think another. If you've been in AA for any amount of time, you've developed a vital sixth sense. You must have a spiritual side to your recovery if you're going to survive living life on life's terms one day at a time. And when it comes to AA relationships, take heed, caveat emptor. Or to keep it simple, buyer beware.

Many 24-Hours

Sonar (sound navigation and ranging) and radar (radio detection and range), are used to determine range and bearing. The technology works by sending out a pulse of energy. It can either be a passive or active pulse. In the active mode, a rhythmic beat goes out and waits for a return. Then, one of three things is probable. There's nothing there. There's something there. Whatever is there isn't seen nor heard. The problem with operating in the active mode is the constant probing discloses the source of the pulse. Thus, the hunter can then be hunted. Not so in the passive mode. In that mode they look, they listen, they wait, they pounce.

Predators know how to manipulate the vulnerable. It's a skill honed long before the terms of gaslighting, ghosting, and trolling came to be. Like any drunk in trouble, they will "yes" you to death to get what they want.

The vulnerable make for the surest score. The stepper, like a U-Boat, stalks about submerged in silence. Spotting a target, the first thing they do is make sure no escort is about. Having all hands-on deck keeping a lookout means if, after launching their 'torpedo' the stepper is detected, a ton of depth charges will rain down upon them. This forces them to the surface. And with being exposed, the only hope of scoring again is moving into a new area of operations.

Like with that first drink, our defense against surprise attack is to maintain constant vigilance and sound the alarm. But let's not get carried away. Many a sighting is a false alarm. There is a spectrum with thirteenth stepping. The stepper that operates only in the active mode is just an asshole. It's the passive stepper that's the sniper. Beware of this one, for they can be both visible escort and unseen as a U-Boat. This makes them the most dangerous of all.

We respect, even look up to, those who have many twenty-four hours. They seem to be able, intelligent, and friendly people. So, when they speak, we listen. But it's from behind the veil of sober normalcy the stepper lurks. So, if we can't control or deny access, then we must internally defend against those that could do our society harm. This is a group effort.

AA is no Shangri-La. We can't stop anyone from coming into our halls. Nor do we want to. Meetings are but a waystation on the road to happy destiny. Not all we meet along the way will be good Samaritans. In fact, for unrepentant evil-doers, AA meetings are their happy hunting grounds.

The most effective, and dangerous thirteenth stepper, is the one who doesn't know they are doing it. These are the ones that cannot be chased away. These are the victims of their own self-pity. Those with a story. The ones who know how to make others feel sorry for them. The stories they tell don't have to be true. They know we would never check. And the longer they're around, the more they believed the illusion and delusion of the lies they tell themselves.

There is no AA Office of Verification. Putting aside that, most of us come in as liars, cheats, and thieves, if someone shows up and says they have twenty years, we believe them. We say it's an honest program, yet how many have you heard say, "My name is XYZ, and I'm an alcoholic rapist."

No one is immune. Be you a crusty old-timer or freshly minted newcomer, there's a thirteenth stepping scammer out there waiting for you. Here's a lesson they taught me at six months of sobriety.

"Charlie" was around a long time and was seen at many a meeting. A power of example he said he was dying. Still, he served. Greeter at this meeting, coffee maker at that one, and treasurer at many more. One day Charlie approached, "Can you loan me fifty till next week? I need medicine." Sure, I thought, I see this guy around all the time. I did not see again him. In addition, the 'prudent reserve' of several groups had likewise disappeared. From that experience, I learned if asked for fifty, give'em five, and call it a gift.

Steppers come into AA from the shady side of the street and the darkest alleys. Nothing attracts a stepper more than a dose of shame, guilt, and remorse. Saying we are only as sick as our secrets don't mean it's safe to broadcast them on all frequencies. Remember, some steppers are sicker than others. These are the parasitic ones. Someone as depraved as they are sick. Thirteen stepping is not an illness; it's a malicious transgression. Defining $E=mc^2$ is much simpler than figuring out the underlying cause of thirteenth stepping. They are more than just maladjusted to life, outright defective, or in full flight from reality. It's a disproportionate dysfunction. Maybe they flunked out of clown school, the nuns slapped their wrist, or they caught it off the toilet seat. They may have a reason. What they don't have is an excuse. And while past performance is no guarantee of future returns, the past is still the best prognosticator of the future.

A symptom of being a dry drunk is acting out like one did when drinking but without the input of alcohol. Many an old-timer falls into this category. They've been around for a long time, but don't get better. They refused to pick up the spiritual tools. Thus, they go on to the bitter end. And yes, you can go on to the bitter end sober. All you need do is blot out of the consciousness an intolerable situation. It's only a question of how many others you take along with you. Sorry, Mr. Newcomer, there are no safe spaces; just ask any altar boy.

The first thing an army recruit is told, "Is know your enemy." This same advice applies to AA. Here is how to identify that Raffle Ticket Romeo. It's your first time speaking, and all you say is,

"I'm Sue; alcoholic." And at once after the Lord's Prayer, you hear, "Nice to hear ya. Wanna go for coffee? I'll show you my Big Book." If this is the case, here's no time for no, just go.

The targets a stepper looks for include:

- Someone who still suffers from a hopeless condition of mind and body.
- Those still rock'en and rolling from the withdrawal of alcohol and drugs.
- The ones who suffer from grave emotional and mental disorders.
- The needy and unwanted.
- Anyone asking, "WTF is going on?"
- The submissive who expects to be beaten down.
- Those with a devil may care attitude. "No worries, I got this."
- Those whose self-esteem is so low they can't get up.
- The people pleasers and enablers.
- The "I'm sorry" types.
- Those with legal, financial, or family troubles.
- Those impaired mentally or physically.

Raffle-ticket Romeos use their charisma to bushwhack the codependent ones. Being taken advantage of is just another hopeless alcoholic trait. Even when forewarned, a potential target can't help touching the hot stove. They don't know how to defend themselves. Wanting to be wanted, they get badly burnt. As a dented can, they hold on hopelessly, to the hope of an unexpected wanting to be wanted reward. They need help to steer clear of being in harm's way.

Making an accusation, especially one about allegedly inappropriate behavior, will put anyone on the defensive. And, as we know, we alcoholics are of the over-sensitive type. Therefore, remember the proverb, praise in public, and question in private. Approaching someone about this matter is best left to those who are impartial. The manner of approach must be calm, frank, and open. We are after a resolution, not confrontation. Do not rely on hearsay. First, it's inadmissible, and second, it's often wrong.

If everybody is only looking for the good in people, nobody will notice who's being bad. Having AA stars in the eye blurs vision. When drunk, if you take your eyes off the road, you'll end up in a ditch. When sober, if you take your eyes off a known stepper, you will end up in the sack.

Introducing Miss. Jane and the First Sergeant (1SG). Every group has one or the other. The safest groups have both. The difference between the two is when Miss Jane asks you how you're doing, she really wants to know. When a 1SG asks how you're doing, they only want to know when you'll be finished. They always have something else for you to do. God doesn't have enforcers of sobriety. So, Miss Jane and the 1SG are God's agents. Their job is to protect you from yourself until you are firmly cemented into the foundation of trusting and relying on God. By keeping an eye on you, they bear witness to God's love, God's power, and God's way of life. They are the escorts a stepper must avoid in the attack.

The purpose of the cavalry is not to charge but to reconnoiter and protect the flanks. Miss Jane is an old-timer and a former nun. She carries a sawed-off yardstick in her crochet bag. With one eye looking left and the other glancing right, the bad guys stay clear of her stare. She tells new girls, "If you want eggs in the morning, don't let a fox in the henhouse at night."

The First Sargent (1SG) goes by the book. This is that guy that can't pass a podium without stopping to say a few words. When they speak, they don't preach; they instruct. They take the personality out of the principles, only reading the black part of our book. There's no reading between the lines with this type. They not only know what the book says, they know what to do. And if you ask them how it works? They'll tell you, one step at a time.

Yes, we say one day at a time, but we really mean forever. And while live and let live may be the rule, when on the firing line of life, you better know how to keep your head down. There's no such thing as a free lunch, and the thirteenth step romance always comes at an exuberant cost.

Under the mask of alcoholism, lurks some severe personality disorders. Alcoholics Anonymous does not treat psychopaths, sociopaths, or sexual predators. For they, like a heat-seeking missile, lock onto targets of opportunity. They know to hit the intended bullseye without being intercepted; they need their victim's help. That's why we have the cavalry on patrol. Our Miss Jane keeps us out of an ambush.

Most AA meetings are co-ed. Hook-ups inevitably happen. Don't let what I say keep you from experiencing sober living. Constant contact with each other is the bright spot of our lives. Millions of AA members have met the love of their lives in the halls. I'm one. I'm only saying be careful. Should the need arise, find Miss Jane. She'll remind you what Dr. Ruth said, "With sex, the most important six inches are the ones between the ears."

While thirteenth steppers don't populate every meeting and are relatively few, they exist. When a stepper approaches, Big Book in hand, be prepared to be "boinked" with it. For they'll be quick to point out we are not the arbitrators of anyone's sex conduct. A Big book in the hands of a stepper is not a tool. It's a weapon.

A practiced stepper can display overwhelming confidence or ooze self-pity simultaneously. This they can do because they are constitutionally beyond the spiritual approach. They find redemption in relapse. Not for themselves, but for their victims. For if the target goes out, they get away with it. After all, who's going to believe a drunk who's been drinking?

The 13th Step is about betrayal and deception. The stepper will often cozy up and befriend before they strike. That's what hurts so much. Never forget who you are dealing with. We are by our own admission liars, cheats, and thieves. Putting the plug in the jug does not come with a dose of ethics. But putting the plug in the jug takes away the alibi that the overindulgence of booze is to blame. This is problematic for those of predatory persuasion that have not yet completely stepped over onto the psychopathic or narcissistic side.

There is a spectrum to thirteenth stepping. It can range from innocuous flirtation to outright felonious sexual assault. There is much in between open to interpretation. One person's pleasure is another's perversion. That is why when the subject of stepping comes up, it's best to go to God at once, talk to someone immediately, and quickly take corrective action. And, while waiting for the right thought or action, relax, take it easy, and do not struggle.

Putting whip cream on horseshit doesn't make it taste any better. If you think you have your shit together, ask yourself what you're doing at an AA meeting. Our primary purpose is to stay sober and help others. Not to "hit on" or "hook up" with anyone that comes through the door. AA is not a barroom without booze. It's a place where a drunken nobody can become a sober somebody. And as Dr. Bob said to Bill Wilson on his deathbed, "Let's not louse this thing up."

Who are these predators? Most stay hidden, but a few work out in the open. It's the latter that is most dangerous. They get away with it because they can. Having a toxic view of the world and its people is not a prerequisite for the thirteenth stepper in training. It's something they develop over time and continue on only because of their success. I read once a master treats their slaves like a slave because a slave has no choice.

It's a canonical truism that what we do speaks louder than anything we say. This observation is the first line of defense in identifying the thirteenth stepper. If you came into AA a liar, cheat, and thief, and after just not drinking for a year or twenty, remain a liar, cheat, and thief, you can't blame booze for that. It's who you are. Like a prosaic steel girder, the spiritually untreated will corrode and return to their old ways.

When a stepper says, "keep it simple," what they really mean is give me what I want. And when a drunk without a drink wants what they can't have, what do they do? They lie, they cheat, and they steal. It worked when they were drinking, so it will work when they're not. Unless they avail themselves of a program of action, a design for living, and a process of recovery. Only by following the clear-cut simple direction can the obsession for alcohol be expelled and allow the practitioner to live a happy, healthy, and whole existence.

And if you don't do the steps? It is hard to say. But there is one thing for sure. If you came into AA a liar, a cheat, and a thief, and just don't drink, you'll remain a liar, cheat, and a thief. Only now you don't have booze to blame for that behavior.

It's God's Job

Sponsorship is not a subservient relationship. It's a partnership. Both you and the new man must walk day-by-day in the sunlight of the Spirit. A sponsor is a mentor. The trainer is preparing the next in line to do what they do. Any sponsor worth their salt takes pride in a sponsee who helps others. And a humble sponsor prepares their protégé to be a better one than they can ever claim to be. A sponsor should train a sponsee as if someone's life depends on it because it does.

The basic sponsorship choice suggestion is men with men, women with women. Regardless of how you slice it, remember two sick ones don't equal a well team. If the sponsor is still sick and the sponsee is not, you'll still have two drunks stumbling about trying to find a way out. The rule, men with men, women with women, is now complicated by a significant LGBTQxyz presence. Here, if unsure, try homo with hetero, or gay with lesbian. Just take heed. Predators are not always male, and not always straight. Like with every aspect of life, buyers beware.

In selecting a sponsor, it's best to shop around and take your time. It's okay to take a test drive with a temporary choice to see how it goes. Jumping from sponsor-to-sponsor wastes valuable sober time. It delays developing a life of trusting and relying on God. If you can't settle down, maybe: (1) There're telling you what you don't want to hear; (2) You're looking for one that will do what you tell them to do; (3) the both of you are only talking about the problem, never the solution. It's okay to get it wrong. As long as you're honest with yourself. If it doesn't feel right, it probably isn't. You're not breaking up, you're moving on. And that is progress. That is the beginning of having clarity of thought,

Many young and old AAs make great sponsors. They've done the work, had a spiritual awakening, and their Big Book falling apart from reading it. Then some should not own a potted plant. Not because they have bad sobriety, can't be trusted, or don't know the difference between the sixth step and a six-pack, but because they obviously cannot transmit something they do not have. Don't grasp onto someone because they are popular, have a nice car, look really hot, have lots of money, or might give you a roll in the hay. Any choice not made solely on trust means its permanency has a shelf-life. Remember, you'll be telling this person *all* your life story. You want to get this right. A good way to start is by hanging out with the parking lot Mafia after a meeting. With that crowd, you'll get a sense of who you might be compatible with because God hangs out with them, too.

Remember, a sponsor's job is not to solve your problems, past, present, or future. Their job is to train future trainers. This they do by bearing witness to your progression, not solving your problems. The third step deal they made is with God, not you. So, unless you have the power to relieve them of the bondage of self, and take away their difficulties. Pay attention to what they say. Remember, in the sponsor/sponsee relationship, you can get along without them, but they can't fulfill the deal they made with God without you.

Many of us come from a culture where we'd rather die than look bad. Asking for help and then doing what we're told to do makes us look bad. This way of thinking you best put aside. For when we say others solve their problems by a simple reliance on the Spirit of the Universe, we had to stop doubting the power of God. Our ideas didn't work, the God idea did. And now that we believe that self-will, self-reliance, and self-knowledge are to no avail? We answer one short question. God either is, or He isn't. What is your choice going to be?

The chapter *Working With Others* supplies a ton of do's and don'ts about sponsoring. But there is little there for the sponsee. This means with deciphering the guidelines, it's the sponsors' word we behold. Now, for ninety-nine-point nine percent of us, this is no issue. Yes, a sponsor may have the sixth step completely ass-backward, but their heart is in the right place. Not so with our cunning, baffling, and powerful thirteenth stepper. When they are out and about, Big Book in hand, rest assured, they are up to no good.

A sponsor's duty is that of a paratrooper pathfinder. They jump in first and mark out the drop zone for the follow-on formations. It's a Pathfinder's job to jump into the unknown and prepare the way for others. AA sponsors are like Pathfinders. They go in first, illuminate obstacles, and ensure you are on the right course. But they won't fight your battles for you.

Here I sometimes get myself in trouble. I believe that after the fifth step, you're technically done with a sponsor. Once they bear witness to your fifth, they're retired. In six and seven, we reaffirm the deal we made with God. We turn our will, the way we think, and our lives, the way we act, over to the care of God. That person who mentored you through the first five steps is now a partner. It's the trainer's job to ensure they train the trainee before they turn them loose. Not to follow them around picking up the pieces. If that's the case, it's one of two things. Your sponsor sucks at being a sponsor, or your sponsor is a part-time unintentional overshadowing stepper. To master the tools of the program requires three things: you, God, and your Big Book. After doing that, you are now ready to trust God, clean house, and help others. That's how it works, so that's what you should do.

Mentorship is not management. We turn our will and our life over to God, not another person. A sponsor is not your life coach. If you're going to them, you're not trusting and relying on God. "Let no one say their recovery depends on another person. It just isn't so. For either God has removed your troubles or He has not. If not, we ask (pray) until He does." And if your sponsor is constantly overshadowing, correcting, advising, and critiquing? They are not mentoring, they're controlling. Our primary purpose is to stay sober. Not to tell anyone who to date, what meetings to go to, where to work or live, or anything else that's not in the book. Understand this; we all have clay feet. That's in the book. The third step deal is with God. He will do for you what you can't do for yourself.

I'm not saying a concerned sponsor is an out-of-control semi-pro thirteenth stepper. What I'm saying is, that humility is standing tall before God, knowing you are who He meant you to be. God is the guardian of your sobriety. You are your sobriety's enforcer. It is what it is, and that's that. Don't you just love First Sergeant talk?

Before proceeding, let's look at that guy hiding behind the curtain. Well, I'll be. It's Bill Wilson.

There had been no real infidelity, for loyalty to my wife, helped by extreme drunkenness, kept me out of those scrapes." (Big Book, p. 3)

Despite what he wrote in *Bill's Story,* any biographical search of Bill Wilson will reveal an unrepentant thirteenth stepper. Remember, our alcoholism is with us drunk or sober, and matter cannot be created or destroyed. It can only change form. One addiction will replace another. There must be an essential psychic change, a vital spiritual experience, and the development of new moral psychology. And for this to happen, we must turn our will, the way we think, and our lives, the way we act, over to the care of a Power greater than ourselves. We used to think one way, and now we think another. Simplicity, clarity, brevity.

Bill Wilson was a compulsive womanizer. His flirtations and his adulterous behavior filled him with guilt, but he continued to stray off the reservation. (Getting Better, Nan Robertson, p. 36)

Bill's peccadilloes resulted in part from his personal popularity. The faithful, waiting to touch his garment, may go a bit too far, but AA has its rock stars. And when there are stars in the eyes, one is easily blinded. However, when God has His eye on you, you get away with nothing. This may explain why Bill suffered debilitating depression until the day he died.

A stepper doesn't want your love. They want power over you. They want you to make them all better. Good luck with that. You're not that powerful.

Intimacy is more than rolling around in the hay doing the deed. It's sharing your secrets and problems. Not so that another can resolve them for you, but so you can be honest with yourself. For if you hide from yourself, how will anybody else be able to find you? Intimacy is consideration, compassion, companionship, understanding, forbearance, and fortitude. That's what we mean when we say, "Love and tolerance of others is our code." Human nature, our wants, and our needs is a two-way street.

Intimacy, like love, doesn't need sex. And while sex without intimacy can be as satisfying as with it, what is a sure bet is sexual satisfaction cannot be stolen. And any satisfaction that may come from theft will be fleeting and soon lost. As we say in *A Vision For You*, the less people tolerated us, the more we withdraw from life itself. The chilling vapor that is loneliness settles down upon us, becoming ever darker, ever blacker. To survive, we seek sordid people, places, and things, hoping to find understanding and love.

If you awake in sobriety to the "shivering denizens" of terror, bewilderment, frustration, and despair, then you need to consider what's the root cause of these disruptive thoughts. Could it be your last three long-term relationships encompassed a three-day weekend? Then again, it could result from living with selfishness or self-centeredness we don't even know we have. A stepper is not born, they're created. They can shift the blame for their shark attack into a "pity-fuck" in the blink of an eye. They betray the trust placed in them, saying, "She's old enough to decide for herself." or "I didn't force her, she asked for it." They may not use alcohol and drugs to lure their prey in, instead, they say all the right things. How does one defend against that?

How about that trust and rely on God thing? They say if you work it. It really works.

Having your wits about you and remembering no good deed goes unpunished will get you by. But only barely. That's the reason we need God as our navigator. He knows the way. He is the guardian of our sobriety. But He's also busy keeping the rings around Saturn and making sure Pluto doesn't slam into Neptune. That's why God puts an annoying Big Book thumper in every group. Not as His "minder", but as a reminder. A thumper won't hit you on the head with the Big Book, but they will show you what page the answer is on. They are akin to a priest with a crucifix facing down a vampire. A Big Book in the vicinity of a thirteenth step in progress drives a spiritual stake into a sobriety-sucking stepper's heart. Seeing Miss Jane or the 1SG coming their way, they'll screw. And as long as the target doesn't follow them, all will be right in the AA world. At least for today, that is.

Some say the Twelve Steps are the production of Providence, and thus perfect. That may be so, but it's impossible to prove. However, what's not impossible to prove is that since Cain slew Able, the capacity for one person to cause harm to another has not diminished. And while we are sure God wants us to be happy, joyous, and free, the world and its people will continue to dominate us. It's a dangerous place for us; drunk or sober.

There is no right way, wrong way, or best way to recover from our seemingly hopeless condition of mind and body. However, what separates man from other creations is reason. This we call self-will.

Ethics is morality. Morals come without effort. The problem is God gives us self-will. It's self-will that makes us fallible to the wanting of earthly pleasures and the avoidance of pain. Just not drinking provides no clarity of thought. Sobriety is a different way of life; a different way of thinking. It's from seeing how we used to live, compared to how we want to live, that the desire to do the next right thing transforms a nobody into a somebody.

When the wreckage of the past washes up on shore, it's no time to let old demons out. Look, none of us are perfect. That's why the rule is progress, not perfection. The reason we need steps ten and eleven is that we're not saints. We're going to make mistakes. We'd hardly be human if we didn't. But such rationalization is not a get-out-of-jail-free card. We must continue to set right wrongs. This is a process that must continue for our lifetime. Yes, in looking back, there may be some wrongs we can never fully right. We don't worry about them if we would right them if we could.

It's okay to let things go if we are painstaking in our development. Do the right things. And make corrections when wrong. Providing we continue to practice our principles in all our affairs. Our program of action, design for living, and process of recovery is for going forward, not looking back. The way to make amends for past, present, and failings to come is to change those behaviors that cause you to say "I'm sorry" in the first place.

If you are sorry for what you have done, and God willing learned your lesson, then all is forgiven. If you think making amends with an old flame means you get to sleep with them again, that amends doesn't count. For if your conduct continues to harm others, you will drink. You'll have to. That's the only way you can get away with it. The only way to shut our heads off and kill the pain is to drink and drug. That's the problem with drugs and alcohol; they work.

But why is this condemnation to drink not fulfilled in the practiced thirteenth stepper? It's because harming others is what they do. They use the same tactics as when drinking, knowing that they will work until they don't. They know how to keep their powder dry and always keep something in reserve. Let's not complicate this. The reason they can get away with it is that they can.

No discussion of humility can proceed far without colliding with questions of what is right. What is wrong? How do we decide? And what we ought to do?

The recovery of an alcoholic "worldview" starts with the question, "God either is, or He isn't. It's on this foundation we place the cornerstone of the arch to which we shall pass to freedom from bondage of self. We used to think one way, but now we think another. This construct of a belief system, we call ethics. This concept is foreign to a devout stepper.

Maslow's Hierarchy of Needs speaks of survival as a bottom-up process. Cicero's Natural Law of Moral Order professes people do the right thing because it's their duty. Confucius teaches that grass bends when the wind blows. In AA, we keep what we have by giving it away. So how do we decide what's the right thing to do? We make a deal with God. In Step Three, we agree that if we do our part, God will do His part.

There are many multitudes of intellectually grounded gobbledygook to define ethics. And what is ethics? It's doing the next right thing. Not because we want to, but because we must. For if we don't practice these principles, we might drink. And for us, to drink is to die. Now that's keeping it simple. A lot simpler than defining epistemology, ontology, and axiology.

That trilogy of big words accurately describes our fourth step. Huh? Let's look at it this way. It's in the resentment part we find out what we're like. In the fear part, why we are like that? And in the sex part, why it's important to change? In each part, we discover and digest some big chunks of truth about ourselves. This, I can assure you, is something the thirteenth stepper will never do. The truth about themselves is the absolute last thing they want to tell themselves. They are the ones who are constitutionally incapable of being honest with themselves.

It's the choice of what we do that separates ethical beliefs and actually acting ethically. What we do speaks louder than anything we will ever say. But nothing is as simple as it seems. It's what Clausewitz calls "the fog of war". This means the needs and wants of living in a bottom-up world easily blinded us. That's why the decision regarding the question of God either is, or He isn't, will define what we'll be like from now on.

It is to this point that we all start out the same. We are outcome-based. This means there is competition for what we are to be. It's the old go-along to get along self, versus the new trust and rely on God's model of acceptance.

Sometimes, fighting off calamity with serenity is like hand-to-hand combat. The surrender of our old ideas, ways, and conceptions must be unconditional. But the old self will never completely or easily let go. It fights dirty and brings a gun to a knife fight. When cornered, it knows all the right things to say to get away. There is no such thing as an unconditional surrender when self-will runs riot. Therefore, we can't surrender ourselves but instead, go to any lengths for *victory* over alcohol.

This we do by turning our thoughts, words, deeds, and actions over to the care of God. Only then will God do for us, what we cannot do for ourselves. This is no extravagant promise. But this isn't what we want to hear. So, that's not what we are going to do. Here we need to be reminded that those who do not learn from their mistakes will repeat them. And if there is one thing alcoholics know how to do, it's doing the same things over and over, and expecting different results. And nowhere is this truer than in relationships where we atone for past mistakes by making new ones.

Let's not complicate this. What makes thirteenth stepping so corrupting is it results from a power vacuum. A vacuum that's not between the stepper and their victim, but between both of them, and God. The stepper defies God's will, and the victim ignores it. The result is a power differential. One where the indifferent manipulation of the vulnerable, impressionable, and naïve is the way the stepper wants it to be. That Raffle ticket Romeo's advice and reassurance (a.k.a. hogwash hocus pocus) has only one intended purpose. For you to drop your guard and let them in.

Everyone's worldview has an intellectual, emotional, and spiritual component. When combined, this is how we live. With sobriety, our worldview changes drastically. We used to think one way and now we think another. Old ideas and conceptions crumble. And upon the ruins, we set a solid spiritual foundation. But what if we skimped on the cement or tried to mix mortar without sand? That's easy to answer. Our foundation will fissure and old ideas and behaviors find their way back in. And in the worst case? The new structure we have built will collapse when ethically challenged.

Our worldview, therefore, must correspond to ethical sobriety. This is doing the next right thing. Thus, two suppositions are necessary. The first is our starting point or cornerstone. And the second is the belief keystone under which we shall live. From these suppositions, we will define what is good and what is bad. And in between the cornerstone and the keystone, we shoehorn not only the world and its people but ourselves.

There is no doubt in my mind that God is eternal, all-powerful, and all-knowing. But one force can circumvent the will of God–that force is self-will. God gave us that power, and it addicted us to let any kind of power go to our heads. The reason I write these books is to prove to the world I'm important. There's nothing wrong with that. God wants us to be happy, joyous, and free. It's acceptable to reach for the stars. Just keep our feet firmly grounded where they are supposed to be and bring no harm to others.

A covenant is a deal. This means it's freely entered, is mutually agreeable, and meant to last. This is what our third step is all about. It's a decision to do the next right thing. But what happens when circumstances shift the groundwork on which we made the contract? Those vicissitudes of life will shake you down, and you'll stumble, fumble, and fall to the ground. You need not worry here. For if God is still your navigator, when flat on your back, everything is looking up.

We are the square pegs in a round hole. Being where you are doesn't mean it's where you're supposed to be. Drunk or sober, there are good guys and bad girls. Acting out and going out is part of the game. Without taking God wherever we go, behaviors and beliefs once considered unethical are suddenly an everyday occurrence. Has the meaning of right and wrong changed? If so, why didn't we get the memo? When we stop trusting and relying on God, self-will runs riot and converts consequential hedonism into motion. Ethics is being qualified, quantified, and turned inside out. For the stepper, fear of other people's opinions is their weakness. For the old-timer whose charisma and standing lets them get away with it, it's their shield.

Understanding the concept of differentiating good from the bad is simple. It's the execution that is complex. For at any point in time, the definition of what is good and what is bad is elastic. This means what's good and what's bad are subject to infinite interpretation. For if something comes before good or after bad, then neither good nor bad can be our starting points. Now, if that isn't some AA psychobabble, I don't know what is. See what I mean, that in keeping it simple, we have to complicate the shit out of everything.

Simply said, if you can't help a drunk, don't hurt them. Instead, spend your time focusing on looking for and improving your conscience contact with God. And everything that forms your worldview will neatly fit between what's good and bad. You don't have to explain it, you'll feel it.

The axiom of utilitarianism requires drawing on the stated principle to argue against that principle. Ethics is not about giving back the extra change. You're supposed to do that. Not, question if you should do that. This we can only reliably do by allowing God to do for us what we can't do for ourselves. Powerless doesn't mean we can't drink. Powerless means we will drink. We will, unless we turn our will, what we think, and our lives, the way we act, over to the protection and care of a God of our own understanding.

Oh, just in case you were wondering?

- Epistemology is how we arrive at the truth.
- Ontology is the study of who we are.
- Axiology is the process by which we change.

And in our fourth step, we discover what we are like, why we are like that, and why it's important to change. See, you can use big words when keeping it simple. We used to think one way, and now we think another. Now that's brevity, clarity, and simplicity.

Be Careful Out There

Microaggressions, triggers, and other snowflake expectations is not thirteen stepping. Harassment is not a one-time occurrence. Rudeness is not intimidation. A wink and a nod in your direction doesn't mean you're being stepped on. If you want to *stay* sober and be happy, joyous, and free, you better learn how to live life on life terms. Or, as President Truman once said, "If you can't stand the heat, get out of the kitchen."

Most "attraction advancement" is innocent and natural. Nothing more than a desire to set the ball rolling by being friendly. Saying "Hi, I like your hat" is no cause for a flamethrower versus snowflake encounter. With sobriety comes flirting. It's normal. And a body without the booze puts the flirtation mode into overdrive. Sober sex? What's that? Which of course leads to the inevitable, "Got any more?" It's like being a teenager again. Then comes those dastardly biological hormones. Screw those principles.

Being free of alcohol, our emotional maturity is on the rebound. Sexual senses awaken. The challenge is thinking, this time will be different, or I know what I'm doing, or I can control it. And once the impervious urge ignites, natural impulses supersede principles. Our thinking goes from everyone looks good at closing time to maybe I'll get lucky. And when this happens, we will succumb. Therefore, we must have God as our shield. God's only job, besides keeping the rings around Saturn, is to protect us from ourselves when we get what we want when we want it.

Drinking retards our sexual development and impairs our judgment. Sobriety is no guarantee this retardation reverses. What it does is bring to light the shame, guilt, and remorse of succumbing to inebriated temptation. Wanting to wipe the walk of shame slate clean, we hump the first one to come along, thinking, "this is the one." Sobriety accelerates our desire to be wanted.

An affection affliction can be addictive too. That rhythmic chugging of I want more makes temptation hard to resist. These phenomena of craving I call the 14th Step.

Why does the 14th step get second billing to the 13th one? Because it turns the victim into the victimizer. That's where we know what is happening and allow it to happen. This we do, despite being warned. Wearing rose-colored glasses makes red flags hard to see.

Words have meanings. And language is the principal weapon of the thirteenth stepper. They are linguistic saboteurs. They say what you want to hear, but what you hear is not what they said. A contronym is a combination of homonyms and antonyms. Better known as double-talk. And what double talk usually leads to is a stab in the back. When only hearing what we want to hear, it's because we are not listening to what's said. This makes it challenging to navigate between pink cloud fantasies and avoiding realities. But then again, what we do speaks louder than anything we say.

The thirteenth stepper knows this. They will use it against you. For the 13th stepper, "attraction advancement" goes like this. Their eyes see it. Their mind wants it. Their hands go for it. And once they get what's wanted; they run from it. Leaving their kill to say, "What did I do wrong?"

This thinking comes from the old self engaging in hand-to-hand gymnastic combat with the new self. Old habits die hard. And yes, you may be a former barfly who "interviewed" the many, but never found Mr. Wright; only Mr. Right now. Don't be too hard on yourself. It's expected, we'll bring with us what brought us here. We know you have a black belt for kicking the crap out of yourself. So, just remember its progress, not perfection.

Going on a date means someone is footing the bill for the movie and a meal. It doesn't mean they own you. And if they think they do, run away. However, in almost all cases, it is what it is, and that's that. And what is that? It's someone being nice to you.

It's understandable if you feel uncomfortable accepting niceness. You think you're not worth it, or experiences prevent it. Here's something to think about. Is it possible you made bad choices but there really are nice people out there? I'm going to say yes, but with a qualification.

An oxymoron doesn't make you a moron. I contend what's wrong with people being nice, is that people suck at being nice. Most of us are just clumsy at something we want to do but don't know how to do it. So, how do you respond to someone being nice to you? Keep it brief, clear, and simple, by *allowing* that someone to be nice to you. However, if being nice is a pretext for getting one's rent paid or dropping their trousers, then remember two lessons found in this book. One caveat emptor. Two, no good deed goes unpunished. So how then do you know what's nice and what's not? It's how you feel after the deed is done.

Then some have no flavor for their fare or are on a straight pepper diet. These are the ones that do not know what they want or what to do. Confused and baffled, they just want someone with a magic wand to come along and "make it all better." This is where the stepper steps in. And even though these types go kicking and screaming when stepped on, they can't muster the strength, nor the sanity, to "just say no." They go along to get along. They just don't know what else to do.

If this sounds like you, then start with this. Check motives. Not theirs, yours. We know what *they* want. It's what you want that causes the hurt. As President Clinton said, "Our deepest wounds are self-inflicted." So, when tempted, ask, are you seeking to steal vicarious pleasure, or is it lust? In differentiating, take the tongue test. It goes like this. When seeing cleavage up to someone's neck, or rolled-up socks in someone's pants, and your tongue hangs out its lust. But if you're dressed as a bag lady, and smoking a burner as if in front of a firing squad and hear the words, "You look great." And you think you do. Be careful what you ask for because you're going to get it. Want it or not?

With thirteen stepping, no group gets a pass. Older straight white men have no monopoly on assholeism. Women can be jerks too. Every race, creed, and color has its share. That's why wherever you go, someone is trying to cut the line. The number of steppers in the LGBTQ community is also rising. This is most troubling to those who remain in the closet. For them, shame, guilt, and remorse come as a double dose. Who can they turn to? Where do they go?

A former director at Hazelden Betty Ford, Melody Anderson, said, "All sexes and gender preferences can be predators." Predators, to get away with what they do, don't have to be cunning, baffling, and powerful; only smart. This makes them all dangerous, all the time.

In psychobabble, the word "boundaries" gets tossed out like pennies in a poker game. Here's how it goes. Establish boundaries and everything is all better now. That's a defense with no substance. Why? We either don't know how to establish boundaries, don't want any boundaries, or are afraid of boundaries.

The defense against a frontal assault differs from that for a flanking maneuver. With the first, you can see what's coming. With the latter, it sneaks up on you. Being asked by an AA'er to go for coffee is one thing, and having that AA'er show up at your apartment uninvited is another. Either way, the danger is the same.

In the defense, the use of obstacles is not to hinder an advance, but to channel the aggressor into the "kill zone". Don't try this with a veteran predator. It's just what they want. It's what they train for. Deceptions and faints are their specialties. They want you to look over there because that's not where they'll be coming from.

Never underestimate the sinister look hiding behind the stepper smile. They know where to look, whom to look for, and what to say before they strike. Learning to establish boundaries, putting them up, and staying behind them requires more than lip service. Remember, a sentry who is scared to death will keep both eyes open. If you look the other way and say nothing, that's the pass go with a get-out-of-jail card free. What we don't say allows them to do what they do. Don't let that stepper get away with that "back rub hug".

Conventional wisdom holds thirteenth stepping is hitting on someone with less than a year of sobriety. Conventional wisdom is often wrong. This definition of the thirteenth step is no exception. There is no magic moment in AA when the light comes on. I know people at ten years sober, who are as naïve on this subject as they were on their last day drinking.

Some get sober and date right away. Others can't even hold their head up. Regardless of which one you are, rest assured, that we all have the same co-occurring disorder. When we drink, we go crazy. And when not drinking? We go bat shit crazy.

When sober, sex is as stimulating an incentive to go to AA as coffee. If we skimp on the cement that binds us to God, we become susceptible to doing things we never thought we would. The spectrum of reactions to a sexual stimulus is determined by the hardware holding those desires in place. Having too many screws loose puts us with people, in places we would not rather be.

Let me make a qualification here. The thirteenth step is not sexual assault, but it can be the precursor. Thirteenth stepping is unethical, even disgraceful, but not illegal. This technicality is a fine line. One you best stay clear of. Especially in your first year.

Provided you are spiritually fit, flirting, dating, and getting to know someone better are not verboten. Constant contact with each other is the bright spot of our lives. Sex is God-given and we shouldn't do without it. It's one cog in the wheel of our return to normalcy, and part of the drive for a white picket fence. But when selfishness and self-centeredness replace godliness, everything gets screwed up. Rehab romances and meeting flings rarely end with happily ever after. Like the survivors of a shipwreck, we're all in the same lifeboat together. Nothing brings individuals together faster than them all going down together. Which brings to mind that eternal relationship question, "How could I have been so stupid?"

Sexual impulsivity is really stupidity on speed. Sobriety can't cure stupid. But we can recover from it. The thirteenth step rule is, here today; gone tomorrow. With the fourteenth step it's, we have met the enemy, and it is us. You can't control being targeted by a stepper, but you have control over being stepped on. If you take the 14th step with the same stepper that took advantage of you last week. We can't help that. That's why we need Ms. Jane, the 1SG, and God to watch over us.

It takes so long to put us back together. Yet, we can fall apart so fast. If you hang around AA long enough, you'll see people with five, ten, or even twenty years drink. And they didn't drink because they were thirsty. They drank because their lives had become unmanageable sober. Being the victim of relationship woes is often cited as relapse justification. That's balderdash! For as the Big Book asks, "did we not ourselves set the ball rolling?" And since the answer is yes, if you go to the 1SG with a relationship excuse in mind, be prepared to hear, "Get off the cross. I need the wood." And in climbing down, you best hope it's not so they can wallop you upside the head with it. For you deserve it.

Golf and sex have scorecards. Alcoholics undercount in one and overcount in the other. In the 1960s, the research team, Masters and Johnson, tried to answer the question, "How many is normal?" The score: three for women; seven for men. What did that prove? They didn't interview any alcoholics.

Now About Sex

You cannot tell what's wrong with something until it breaks down. With sex, most of us needed an overhauling there. There weren't that many. It was all plain vanilla. Nothing kinky. Nothing wild. Nothing to worry about because it was all done before and will all be done again. Our participation often nothing more than just being there. Yet, sex is something we think about it all the time. How do I look? Am I fat?

Why is sex part of the fourth step? It's because with or without the consumption of alcohol, a quick fix hump and dump tells us we're okay. A giggle, a smile, a wink, and a nod ignite a sense of wow! We do insane things to satisfy this impervious urge. And if it works? We want more. And if it doesn't? Well, we just want more.

With troubling sex, most pain is self-inflicted. This is to be expected when the consumption of alcohol, or the lack thereof, mixes with libido in ideal. We are not in this manner much different from the non-alcoholics. "But drinking does complicate sex relations."

The sex part of the fourth is about relationships. It's where we discover why it's important to change. And how's that done? We review our conduct over the years. "We got this all down on paper and looked at it." It's this dark cranny of the past, that our serial stepper never looks at. So, their housecleaning is never complete. And what happens if your housecleaning is not complete? Then the equation of trust God, clean house, and help others cannot be solved. This is why the stepper has difficulty changing their ways.

Our darkest secrets are the ones we are ashamed of. Yet we are told to "cling to the thought that the dark past is the greatest possession you have. With it, you can avoid untold misery for yourself and countless others." In the sex part, these are the questions we ask.

- Where had we been selfish, dishonest, or inconsiderate?
- Whom did we hurt?
- Did we unjustifiably arouse jealousy, suspicion, or bitterness?
- Where were we at fault?
- What should we have done instead?
- We subject each to the test: is it selfish or not?

This work is not to punish you. For sex is God-given and therefore good. This makes the sex part about developing a future sexual ideal. Here we neither regret the past nor shut the door on it. In the sex part, it's not all bad.

Sexual pressure is induced at an early age. From Sesame Street to death's door, sensuality and sexuality are everywhere. Why do we buy something? It fulfills the void of want. And nothing can fix a dented self-esteem faster than being wanted. And when we want something bad enough, we take the risk, wish upon a star, and hope for the best. What usually happens? The show doesn't come off that well.

In advertising, sex is the hook. It grabs attention. Madison Avenue paints a picture of being happy, joyous, and free. Advertising tells us to hurry up and grow up. Sexual indoctrination, inoculation, and exploitation say our body is a commodity to be bartered for. And once we get a taste, what do we want? We want more.

Being out and about having one after another is the harbinger of the more yet to come. When sober, a forty-year-old dad bod on a twenty-year-old frame doesn't get a second look. However, when drinking until two in the morning, everybody looks good at closing time. That unemployed felon with ten years of unpaid child support who bought you several drinks—now that's a keeper. What were you thinking? You'll soon find out.

To fill the void of more, we need someone with a shovel. And putting one more log on the fire means it never goes out. Two newcomers flirting, dating, moaning, and groaning fuel and feed the fire of need. Given the fragile state of first-year sobriety, we'd go out with a trashcan if we thought they filled it with what we wanted. This is the volatile dynamic of two drowning sailors. In trying to save themselves, each grab on to the other. This way, they can go down together.

The central sex organ is the brain. When stimulated, the libido fires on all cylinders. It chugs along to a rhythmic chant of; I want more; I want more; I want more. When out of your mind, the voices in your head get very loud, very fast. And what do those voices say? I want more. It's the compulsion of affection: that dangling shiny object, the proof you're not a dented can. The want to be wanted is uncontrollable. That's why the intake of alcohol turns off inhibitions and lowers expectations. When an attraction is sex-based, the eyes see it; the mind wants it, and the hands go for it.

What does drinking have to do with sex? Nothing. But turning the question around the answer is quite different. This reversal is like the observation that every time you drank, you didn't get in trouble. Yet, every time you got in trouble; you were drinking. Many women are drunk the first time they have sex which explains a lot about who they had it with. For me, if it wasn't for a bag of pot, a six-pack of Schlitz, and a '67 Bel-Air, I'd still be a virgin.

Why does sex seem better before the act than after? Could it be something was missing? If our sex powers are God-given, why then don't we feel good every time? Could it be you're trying to wrest, or take by force, that which is not given? Yes, all good things come to those who wait, but for us, waiting is just something we don't do. Wait a year? Are you f-ing out-of-your-ever-loving-mind?

Can you thirteen step yourself? Sure. Most of us do and are so good at it, that we don't even know it's happening. Think about all those selfies you take. A self-actualized 13th step is when the short-term relief is chosen over long-term pain. Remember that drunken half-naked pose your ex-boyfriend said he'd delete? Yeah, that's the one that always pops up whenever you try to send a serious tweet.

Bonding in AA happens. There's the camaraderie type, the fraternal type, the extramarital type, and the "I hate that M-F type." Still, we are all in this together. That's how it works for us who have tried everything else. To prove this point, how do you feel when you see an "I'm a friend of Bill" bumper sticker? For a moment, you feel good about yourself, no matter how much you think you suck.

Sweeping the room, eyes lock. That's it, you're done, put a fork in it. In a nanosecond, you've romanticized, sexualized, and fantasized a passing glance. In the blink of an eye, your hypothalamus goes from "I suck", to, "They want me." It matters not that a blink of the eye is exactly how long that locking glance lasted. Is this proper or not? That's personal. We stay out of this debate. "We all have sex problems; we would hardly be human if we didn't." Note the word is have, not had.

Still, it doesn't matter what you think, it's about what you want. And what do you want? You want more of whatever makes you feel good. That's why sexual fantasy is a go-to substitute. Why? Because we want what we want when we want it, and instant gratification takes too long. We will pay any price to feel satisfied. And that is something that rarely, if ever, happens with people like us.

It's advised to refrain from major changes in the first year. Great advise, rarely followed. That's because of the co-occurring disorder that accompanies alcoholism. Which is, when told what to do, we go crazy. And why do we go crazy? Because our alcoholism is with us drunk or sober. It's an Alcoholic Axiomatic Law of Illogical Thinking (AALIT) that an alcoholic will never do what they are told to do, and always do what they are told not to do. The reason we ignore good advice that's for our own good is because we want what we want when we want it.

The first sober battle you'll encounter will not be with the bottle, but the clock. You'll think there's nothing to do because you're doing nothing. That's the good news. The bad news is you may have a sober body, but you still have an alcoholic mind. That's where the internet comes in. There, instant gratification, compassion, understanding, and love awaits. All that you want, real and imagined is but a few keystrokes away. Behind that wall of electrons, Nigerian princes and mail order Russian brides await. The 13th step is not the sole domination of AA.

Unlike the bars and clubs where we wiped our feet on the way out, AA's doors are never locked. Everyone is welcome and no one gets tossed about. AA is the place, where no matter what kind of nut walks through the door, we have a wrench to fit. We offer a solution, a way out. That's way oldies, newcomers, and all in between, look forward to going to "their meeting." It's kind'a like when we passed out on the floor at *Cheers,* everybody knows our name.

Relationships are easy to get into and hard to get out of. Most relationships end after sex than before. Drunk or sober, it's tough to have an intimate relationship when you keep pushing people out of your life. However, a sane and sound sexual ideal is attainable. Despite its thorns, a rose does bloom.

Relationships are living creations. We must nurture them to achieve maturity. You don't age out of a desire for sex; you become more selective. There is nothing more romantic than an elderly couple holding hands. Make sex the base and not the height of a relationship.

Love is not for the fainthearted. It's baptism under fire. There's no way around it. It's more trial and error than love and tolerance. That's why so many of us only know how to get in, then get out, before being found out. That's why sex with the lights on without booze in the system scares the shit out of us.

A genuine relationship takes attention to detail, consistency, reliability, honesty, and open communication. If you're told what to do, how to do it, when to do it, and who to do it with, without good reason, you're being taken advantage of. If one is trying and the other coasts along, the sum of the whole is a half-measure. And what does a half measure get us? Nothing. And what does nothing mean? It means what my chemistry teacher told me my effort got me. That would be an F, zero, no credit, and no partial credit. If your idea of a long-term relationship is a three-day weekend. Then maybe you need to take another look at the sex part of your fourth step.

We construct lasting relationships from the ground up. Trying to assemble one without directions leaves plenty of parts left over. And while life doesn't come with a manual. Alcoholism does. The steps are not just about detoxing. They are about being rid of unwanted behaviors. Our twelve steps are a program of action, a design for living, and a process of recovery that seem to work with people like us. And who are the people like us? We are the alcoholics of the hopeless variety. For if you're an alcoholic, and not hopeless, you don't get to Alcoholics Anonymous. And just as important, the reason we stay, is because our alcoholism is with us drunk or sober. Here's the short-form directions on how it works.

1. We admit
2. We believe
3. We decide
4. We write down facts
5. We find forgiveness
6. We become ready
7. We make the leap
8. We have a list
9. We set things right
10. We keep a look out
11. We go about our day
12. We give it all back

A shaky hand cannot still a troubled heart, and a ruptured heart cannot remain unrepaired. We all have holes in our hearts. When there is a leak, it needs to be plugged. Heart holes are heart-shaped. This means only God can plug them. That is where these steps come in.

As we enter the world of the Spirit, we recall why we relied heavily—and exclusively—on drugs and alcohol in days gone by to cope. It's because they worked. Now, that we are clean and sober we still need something to get us through the day. Regardless of how spiritually minded we think we are; our human nature remains intact. That's why we need to go to meetings. For it is there we learn how to maintain our spiritual condition. Meetings provide us with more than just not drinking. They provide: A path to healthy living; A deviation from past depravations; Instruction on how to reconstruct a life, and; Reconciles the past, so we can move into the future.

There's the idea that when we stop drinking, we return to the emotional age where it all began. Being damaged goods, dysfunctional urges and fantasies, are seen as opportunities lost. All we want is a second chance at another second chance. Continuing along the path toward perpetual and permanent sobriety, requires clarity of thought. However, when the impervious urge erupts, clarity of thought is in short supply.

A person engaging in 13th step behavior understands weakness and vulnerabilities. Their power comes from capitalizing on yours. They can only take what you give them. And once you give them a taste, they devour all of you. This leaves nothing for anyone else. That's why thirteenth stepping at a meeting is such a dastardly violation of trust.

The particularly susceptible are like Hansel and Gretel. They leave a trail of crumbs for the wolf to follow. No matter how hard they try they can't get out of harm's way. They seem to be in a constant state of shell shock displaying the thousand-yard stare. "Thank you, sir. I'll have another!" They are such unfortunates. After detoxing from their drug of choice they need a new drug. And what do we do when we want what we want? We go looking for more.

And if you fall into a 13th step trap? You don't have to drink. God willing, you've learned a lesson and not only will you not repeat, your experience will prevent it from happening to others. God will take you to better things. But we must be willing to grow towards it. This is where the stepper falls short. They just can't imagine the part they play in anything is to be sorry for. After all, they got what they wanted, therefore, it must have been the right thing to do.

The directions for shaping a sound sexual ideal are clear. We pause and pray. You don't have to get all elaborate and evangelical in doing this. Simply use the sex prayer from our fourth step.

> *God, I pray you mold for me my sexual ideal.*
> *To give me guidance in each situation.*
> *Grant me the strength and the sanity to do the right thing.*
> *Thy will not mine be done.*

Going to God for guidance before is always more gratifying than asking for forgiveness after. When we place our relationships wants in God's hands, everything we want, always turns out better than anything we could have imagined.

She'll Have Another

To paraphrase Psalm 37:8, don't give in to worry, anger, or the impervious urge; it only leads to trouble.

Don't touch the hot stove. Keep your distance. Don't walk into a minefield. Don't eat any yellow snow. We universally suggest, making no major changes in the first year. And when we receive a suggestion, we don't want to hear it; we reject it.

Some people throw pennies away, others pick them up. We look for the perfect soulmate and when we don't find what we want; we take what's left. Some say relationships in early recovery only led to trouble. Others prescribe the mindset: "What the hell, what's one more dent?" Here's a test: Get a potted plant. You can get a pet if that does not die. If that lives, you can think about going on a date. If you survive the first one without getting drunk, then you might have a chance for a second one.

Self-gratification at the expense of others, sexually or otherwise, is thirteenth stepping. It always comes at a cost. It may only be a penny's worth, but eventually, pennies add up. What we do speaks louder than anything we say. And what we say sounds the loudest when we are trying to deny what we know we did. Unless you are the most psycho of the sociopaths, you get away with nothing.

The sexual experience changes a relationship. If it didn't, you could have sex with your friends. Affection fantasy is often the first addiction. Your first love becomes an obsession. And as soon as we capture the love of our lives, we plan our escape. Why? It's those damn expectations.

It's the setting up of expectations that acts as the primer that sets off an unexpected detonation. It's expectations that separate love from sex. When sex competes with love, it's never enough, not the right kind, or not satisfying. When love is conditional, it always disappoints. Being in love does not need sex and sex does not equal love. It's also true no unsatisfied sex for love experience is complete without self-humiliation. And what distinguishes sex from love is that dreaded c-word: commitment.

The two most disappointing days of the year are Valentine's Day and Christmas. Why? Because of expectations, we put on others to make us happy. If you are always telling yourself you suck, what makes you think others can make you happy? Self-flagellation with "suck-ness in progress" does not confirm the conclusion that everybody sucks. Only that you do. Trying to seize happiness from others only results in disappointment in yourself.

Some things are proportional to each other, and some are not. In mathematics, the inverse of the positive is the negative. It's a rule that whenever a positive is multiplied by a negative, the product is always less than zero. Alcohol and drugs bring people into our lives. Addiction chases them out. So, if you keep score, remember disappointment is always one point ahead. This is where Milo's Law of Expectations will always save the day.

Huh? What's that? Well, it starts with an observation. One made unequivocally and without fear of contradiction—people suck. And why do people suck? It's because they never do what we want them to do. And why would we think people should do what we want them to do? In a word, expectations. Keeping that in mind, here's Milo's Law of Expectations:

I am never disappointed in people. Because I fully expect to be disappointed by people. Therefore, the only time I'm disappointed in people is when they don't disappoint me.

Living by this rule puts peace of mind in hand. I guarantee it. Try it. What have you got to lose? The worst thing that can happen if it doesn't work? You'll be disappointed in me.

Affection fantasy is the primer that sets off the expectation detonation. Be it a last-call romance or first meeting fling, you're walking into a minefield. One where the mine doesn't explode until you step away. Ignoring this warning gets you blown to bits again. And again.

We are known for what we do, not what we want to do. Being humble, it's progress, not perfection. In completing the fifth step, we get no halo. What we get is a chance to start over. And while God removes our defects of character, He doesn't remove our human nature. And if you get a halo? Just remember that halo above your head is only inches away from becoming a noose around your neck.

AA is a fellowship of individuals. People who would not ordinarily mix. Because if we did while drinking, it would have been one helluva drunken orgy and brawl. Having shared the consequences of an alcoholic life. There is camaraderie among us. One which is indescribably wonderful.

A common definition of the 13th step is *exploitive or predatory* behavior that harms others. It's not a light-hearted, flirtatious, or natural attraction to another person. Attraction is not harassment. Flirting doesn't earn one a 13th stepper label.

Still, not everyone is comfortable with a light-hearted, flirtatious approach. If you're offended by innocent intent, remember alcoholics are sensitive people. And if light-hearted attention triggers you. Ask yourself who is holding the gun. The probable answer is, that it's you.

Addicts instinctually know when danger lurks. We get away with what we get away with because we know how to get away with it. Wallowing in the trenches of addiction, gut feelings and premonitions develop. Unfortunately, when we get that feeling of 'don't go in there—we go right in. We just can't help ourselves. We get a thrill out of not being blown up, and a bigger thrill out of getting blown up. Damned if we do, damned if we don't. It's just what we do. That is until we let God take charge. The blood spilled in the war on drugs and alcohol is as real as found on a battlefield. Drugs and alcohol play for keeps. Sometimes the best we can do is not get worse.

"Come on down!" For those new to recovery, the AA dating game is the surest way to relapse. When fascination strikes and allure takes over, those with relationship addictions cascade from one target to another. Spinning about in random orbit within the intensity of the obsession, many pass through the crosshairs of the bullseye, certain a moving target is harder to hit. Then, barely escaping the hangman, they sleep under the guillotine, falsely believing that exchanging the noose for the blade somehow makes it "all better now."

Fresh out of last-call hook-ups, alcoholics turn to rehab romances, first-meeting flings, and dented can relationships to make their lives "all better now." In bars, rehab, and AA, the vulnerable mingle. The vitality of sober lust morphs into an unwavering twenty-eight-day hostage-taking fling. It's a placebo effect. Early sobriety relationships stay committed until something better comes along.

That's only fair. They, like you, are heavy-hitting romance warriors too. They better be. Because sexual relationships in early sobriety mean you're going to get your emotions crushed, brains bashed in, and heart ripped out.

FILO is inventory jargon for first in, last out. The first addiction is usually the last to go. Love fantasy is often a young girl's first drug of choice. It's the dream of wanting to be wanted. And when someone wants you, there is a gush of power. Many alcoholics have an affection addiction too. It's codependency, carried out between the sheets. That's why Miss Jane tells her girls, "The only thing a woman needs between her legs in the first year is her Big Book."

Typically, first-meeting relationships spell disaster. It's the old three-minute hump and dump rule. Three minutes to fall in love, three for the act, three to regret it all, and three to call it quits. And for a man, three more to get over it. Lust and codependence are not the ingredients of a stable relationship. If your love obsession becomes your Higher Power, you're in for a crash landing. Be careful, by the end of your first month sober, you could fall in love with a trash can.

We *get sober* by saying yes. We *stay sober* by saying no. However, even though "no" is the first word we learn, as we get on in age and experience, we become more reluctant to use it. Why? Fear of other people's opinions. We want to be wanted. We want to be liked. We can't take care of ourselves because we're focused on helping others. When a stepper doesn't hear no, they think you said yes. This is just the way they like it. If you doubt this "just say no" strategy is proper, remember this line out of our book. "Our troubles are basically of our own making."

In 2011, the CBS network broadcast *The Sober Truth*. It was a tale of two stories. The first boy meets a girl on the AA campus. The second, no good deed goes unpunished.

The protagonist was a young woman with a drinking problem. The antagonist is a man with a secret. Both had been "sentenced" to attend AA. There they sobered up together, fell in love, and got engaged. It looked like another AA success story. Then the truth came out. But not before the brutal murder of the bride-to-be by her betrothed. For he, was a convicted rapist with a violent history. This the court knew. How ironic that in putting these types in a place they don't want to be, it turns out they found a target-rich environment. This is but one story like this where a dream turns into a nightmare.

That's why it's imperative Ms. Jane and the 1SG, watch, look, and listen. We all know "that guy" who has long-term sobriety but doesn't have a clue why. To them, as long as they are just not drinking, they are doing everything right. They read the tenth step as the, I can do anything I want to step as long as I say I'm sorry.

For them, the solution is in words traced back to 1550. "There, but for the grace of God go I." Words spoken when an innocent man was executed. Historical note: they later burned the originator of those words at the stake for blasphemy. Proving once again, that no good deed goes unpunished.

You're supposed to have a choice to have sex or not. Being drunk dilutes that facility. When drunk, it's more about the doing rather than who you did it with. We know why you do it. First, it's sex, for God's sake. And second, there is the excitement of expectations. Nobody wants to be a dented can. So, the harder question to answer is why do you always feel better about sex before the act than after? It's because after we must answer, was it to help, to hurt, to get, to give, to run, to be, to hide? Was it selfish or not? Or was it yes to all? You couldn't help it. Neither could we. That's why we are not the arbitrators of anyone's sex conduct.

A relationship between consenting adults is more than a yes or no. There are limits and benchmarks too. One may see it this way, but the other sees it that way. Like being in a conflicting crossfire, every second it becomes more confusing. The miscommunication of words, hand signals, and body language can't save the day. For one says, "Wanna fuck?" And the other hears, "Would you like to go for coffee?"

Consent doesn't mean going along out of fear or the belief that if you go along, we'll all get along. Consent is a contract. A contract is more than an agreement. In legal terms, for a contract to be valid, something more than words counts. No contract exists without "consideration." And what is that? Consideration is what each party gives to the other. So, in making the offer, the receiver must know: (1) there is an offer, (2) what the offer is (3) what's under "consideration" in the exchange, and (4) there's a right of acceptance or refusal.

It's not that we're not aware of the need for no. It's that we let our guard down. So, we get knocked to our knees, are on the mat, and down for the count. This is great news. Here, our expectations have finally beaten us into a state of reasonableness. After all, when flat on your back, everything is looking up.

We can find the nuances of sexuality in friendly, innocuous banter. No harm done. However, if the conversation shifts to an inquisition, beware. Inquisitive probing on subjects considered out-of-bounds is just that. Any offer to meet in an out-of-the-way secluded spot is a red flag moment and you better check your six.

In case you haven't noticed up to this point, I use a lot of military jargon to get an idea across. This is for two reasons. One, the concepts are tried and true and tested. And two, I'm a retired army First Sergeant paratrooper and air traffic controller. Both professions make me good at telling others where to go and what to do. Taking on a practiced thirteenth stepper is risky. For they, after many years of being on the prowl, have been there, done that, and probably got a mug-shot or two. It's one thing to be armed with the facts about yourself and quite another to defend yourself. In reacting to a bushwhacking, bra-grabbing, 13th step hug attack, deploy these weapons.

The Dirty Look - One of the most effective defenses on the first pass is the dirty look. This takes skill because not just any dirty look will do. An effective dirty look must be like a harpoon. The stepper's got to think, "My God, if that hurt so bad going in, just imagine what it's going to feel like coming out." Now, go find a mirror and try out your best dirty look. CAUTION: if your dirty look makes you smile, it will not work. For the thirteenth stepper only sees, hears, and thinks what they want to see, hear, and think. A dirty look that makes someone laugh is no dirty look at all. Instead, it's an invitation.

Shot Across The Bow – For those who cannot master the dirty look, the next best thing is a verbal and body language shot across the bow. Here it's all about timing and taking good aim. This is how this technique works. Sensing the sleaze hug coming, first step back. Next, point finger. Third, pull verbal trigger. Like a timely, "Thy will be done," a well-aimed, "Get the fuck away from me!" is never a waste of ammo.

Escalate To Deescalate – In case the shot across the bow is ineffective, be prepared to "go nuclear." There's no second guessing with this one. The reason the USSR and USA never fought a war was because of the fear of Mutually Assured Destruction (MAD). This option is fatal for the 13th stepper. Remember, they need to get in and get out before being found out. When under attack, jump up and down, yell and scream, point the finger, and call in the Ms. Jane cavalry and 1SG armor. The more public the nuking, the more effective it will be. You'll know if "going nuke" was appropriate. The stepper won't show up again in the aftermath of you going MAD on them. The fallout is too great.

Moving Target – If there is one thing most alcoholics are good at, it's getting out of Dodge. When it comes to getting caught, a moving target is always harder to hit. While this sounds easy, it's not. Why? Because a stepper is an expert and you're not. Ask any fishing person and they will say trolling is the most effective way to catch fish. Why is this? A fish with its mouth open always takes the bait. Everyone wants to be told, "Nice to hear ya. You're so deep. You look great."

Mostly, it's innocent banter to break the ice. But when you're the target, kind words are used to lure you in. If you're in search of nice things to be said about you, you're setting yourself up to be shot like a fish in a barrel. So, if you're one of us who has the gift of gab, beware about getting reeled in. A fish with a closed mouth can't get hooked. And if you're not hooked, you can get away. If you're always being reeled in, it's because you take the bait.

Cover and Concealment – A sniper must stay hidden to take the shot. To avoid being shot, the target best hides. Going to a meeting dressed to the nines sends a message. It may not be the one you want to be transmitted. A stepper will hear. All you need to please is me. Some of us can't help ourselves. We must go looking for trouble. This is how we operate when wanting what we want. And like what happened at the Come Again Lounge come morning, your car is nowhere to be found. So, the best way to stay out of the crosshairs of the bullseye is to be passive. Don't make yourself a target. An ounce of prevention is worth a pound of cure. Capeesh, understand, entender, 古, got it?

Escape And Evasion – While this may sound similar to cover and concealment, it's not. It's not, because it's working in the active mode. Here, getting out of the line of fire requires instinctual reactions. A seasoned soldier can hear an incoming round and hit the deck while the "new guy" stands around and gets blown to bits. So, if approached and you get that gut feeling that something is wrong, do these three things. Run away, run away, run away!

Use Them to Lose Them – "If you wrong us, do we, not revenge?" Is your toilet backed up? Car won't start? Need to move? Want to get even? A seasoned stepper can fix anything. The "I'm a handyman" line, is their ticket to get in your door. Bitching about that backed-up toilet is chum for the sharks. And the best way to repel any future shark attacks is to have Ms. Jane and the 1SG waiting there with you when they arrive. They'll watch them, and you'll get your toilet to flush. It's a win, win, for the good guys.

A2D2 is not a cute, funny drone. It stands for Area Access Defense and Denial. It's a serious defensive military strategy. We all use defense mechanisms to cope with the inevitable broken shoelaces of life. But coping doesn't mean escaping. That's the concept of A2D2. If you can't discourage, then prevent. If you cannot prevent, then enforce. Keeping an air of A2D2 when near a suspected stepper can yield the following results.

- Recognizes the risk/reward ratio
- Reduces the likelihood of a surprise attack
- Nips one in the bud if begun
- Assesses and reports the battle damage
- Cuts losses and stops the bleeding
- Supplies intel on the attacking force
- Allows others to prepare their fortifications
- Let's you maneuver out of the way
- Brings down overwhelming counter-battery fire
- "Fire for effect", sends them running for the hills

The laws of physics dictate the predictability of cause and effect. Drastic measures need drastic action. Like with drinking, the 13th step is a zero-sum game. Once is enough. However, before you call in "fire for effect" you best make sure the rounds are going to fall on the right target. And always remember, according to Ms. Jane, "Recovery isn't found in between the hips and thighs."

Doveryay, No Proveryay

The phrase a stepper fears the most is the Russian proverb "Trust, but verify."

Beware of conditional friendships. A proper AA hug does not come with a back rub. AA is a mixed bag of nuts. We, like the army, will take any screwball that walks through the door. The bad news is, that not everyone is a volunteer. And the good is God has a wrench to fit everyone that does. If you ask anyone who's been around a while how it works, they'll tell you just fine. Provided of course, none of us are in charge.

A key ingredient in mixing up a hodgepodge of harmony is agreement. A central tradition of the fellowship is unanimity. Agreement on what unanimity is depends on what is acceptable. This makes harmony fleeting and soon lost. Doubt this? Go to any group-conscious business meeting with your fantastic ideas on how to make AA better. They'll show you what love and tolerance are; not.

Sobriety and civility are balancing acts. We often go along to get along. And for a group that knows their Miranda Rights, this is quite an accomplishment. When told we can remain silent, we can't shut up. And when told anything we say can be used against us. We scream at the arresting officer, "Go fuck yourself!" So, we ought not to talk behind a member's back. Even face-to-face accusations are discouraged. We leave it up to the individual to say who they are and how they're doing. We stress it's an honest program. Yet, I've never heard it said, "Hi my name is XYZ and I'm an alcoholic and serial thirteenth stepper."

To work, SX4 (spirituality, sobriety, sanity, and serenity) requires loyalty. This means to God, our fellows, and our society. It's a loyalty that extends to the innocent and guilty alike. This leaves the flanks of our fellowship exposed to attacks from within our ranks.

Drinking will never disrupt a group's unity. But group dysfunction and moral bankruptcy will. When infected by gossip, criticism, and accusations, group members divide. This is because most of the time what's said is inappropriate or an outright lie. AA only works when we put our principles before our personalities. This means WAIT (Why Am I Talking?). This *alcohonyism* has three questions. Does it need to be said? Does it need to be said by me? Does it need to be said by me now?

Can you go to AA for thirty years and be a dry drunk? Sure, why not? But if the question is why? Then the answer is one we know all about. We want what we want when we want it. And if we don't get what we want? We upend and turn everything inside out.

Monica Richardson is one such person. She was in the fellowship for thirty-six years. In 2011, she left not because she wanted a drink, but as a protest. In her view, sexually predatory behavior in

AA was "systematic" and "condoned". Not being able to WAIT she produced a sixty-minute documentary film, *The 13th Step* (2016).

On first viewing, *The 13th Step* looks like a hatchet job on AA. One made by a disgruntle AA woman all the steppers passed over. Many of the presenters in her film are non-alcoholic professional types. These are doctors, therapists, academics, and lawyers who know all about AA, despite never going to a meeting. There are also some who, for reasons I will not criticize, came to AA and found it not for them. All sing the same song. AA is for losers, who learn how to live life on life's terms, from losers.

You can get to know Monica through her YouTube videos. I would suggest that while Monica's delivery may rub some the wrong way her intent was not to hurt AA but to save it. You don't stay sober for thirty-something years a suddenly wake up thinking it doesn't work. From what I can gather her beef was not with AA but with our boundaries. Here's the story. Boy meets girl on AA campus. Boy murders girl he met on AA campus.

Richardson's film tells us what we already know. Individuals charged with sexual crimes are ordered to attend meetings. Most resent their "sentencing" to AA. However, after a meeting or two, they realize they found their happy hunting grounds. AA has no warning they are coming. And would not stop them, even if they were.

There is an axiom that no good deed goes unpunished. A sexual predator being court-ordered to AA is manna from heaven. What *The 13th Step* is about is, that we let everybody in, and don't throw anybody out. This means our dirty laundry doesn't get washed. We can't, nor should, we push these memories aside hoping they never see the light of day. We can neither keep it a secret nor shout it from some moral hilltop.

Critics of AA say AA is cult-like, and the Big Book, our bible. Unfortunately, once a big lie takes root, it becomes gospel. Advocates for victims want "AA's leaders" to identify perpetrators. And are suggestive that there be zero tolerance in our tolerance code. This we cannot do.

Learning the lexicon of AA is pretty easy. Walking the walk, not so much. The problem with group work is having to do it with other people. Why? Because we are spiritual beings trying to live in an imperfect world with people like us. What that means is wherever we go, someone like us will be there. Complete with all their foibles, failures, and fumbles. We're not saints.

Preying on someone is not the same as praying for them. The accomplished 13-stepper will say ignore that man behind the curtain. Look over here. See all the good work we are doing? Anyone who says otherwise? Well, they're lying. A solid-looking tree may appear to be all good on the outside, but that doesn't mean there's not a lot of rot going on inside. Claiming to be something you're not in a life and death errand is stolen valor. It's one thing to know what to say, and quite another to know what to do.

Washington D.C.'s oldest and largest AA group is the Midtown Group. The Midtown Group meets a dozen times a day at multiple locations. It claims three hundred members. Its "leader", Mike Q., calls it the "franchise." It's more like a syndicate. For when it comes to one bad apple, it's alleged the Midtown AA Group is one rotten bunch.

In 2005, after eleven alcohol and psychiatric hospitalizations, she finally found a solution. It was AAs Midtown Group. She didn't find it strange that as a newcomer, she was told to only go to Midtown meetings.

At her first meeting, a sponsor was "assigned". It was a much older man. Can you say, "red flag"? Her "sponsor" also prohibited her from taking any mood-altering drugs. Prescribed or not, this was chewing her booze. There was also a mandatory cut-off from anyone, not a member of "our group." This included friends and family. Any contact with an outsider had to be chaperoned. At fifteen, she was safe. At sixteen, the age of consent in DC, she became "fair game".

In 2007, Newsweek Magazine ran an investigative report of Midtown's alleged cult-like practices. Think about that. This story broke in a nationally distributed news magazine! For millions of people, this would be all they would ever know of AA. And as they say in the biz, "But wait there's more."

All members were regularly reminded of the seventh tradition. Putting a buck in the basket was not enough. Self-supporting meant only renting apartments from group landlords. Need some groceries? Only go to Mike Q's approved stores. That beneficiary on a life insurance policy? It better be the group. Feeling lonely and want to go out and do something? Well, that's approved. As long as you go with who we say. This is all for your own good you know? You can trust us. We're not like the others.

Most Midtown members were newcomers. So, only attending Midtown sanctioned meetings, seemed normal. Our young gal felt welcomed. She put the plug in the jug. In fact, her psychic condition improved. She told anyone who asked, that she felt safe and wanted to stay a member of the Midtown Group. She would later call this the worst decision she ever made.

The particulars of what happened next are irrelevant to this work. You can find out all you want with an internet search. What is of relevance, is our own awareness of, and reaction to, a thirteenth step occurrence in our own group.

When approached by Newsweek, AA, except for an inference to Traditions Four and Ten, had no comment. The fourth tradition relates to each group being autonomous. And the tenth is that AA has no opinion on outside issues.

I get where AA is coming from. With 180,000 groups in 180 countries, and no leaders, except for Mike Q., what can they do? This, if ain't broke, don't fix it philosophy, seems to work with people like us. And who are the people like us? We're just a bunch of drunks who aren't drinking and who have adopted the use of a book published in 1939. This the courts have also found to be true. Thus, AA has no criminal responsibility for who does what under the banner of AA.

Still, there is the civil side of jurisprudence. Lawsuits brought against AA often cite the judicial primacy that AA has a "duty to warn." And in not doing so, "have a reckless disregard for, and deliberate indifference." To date, AA has been found to have no standing in that matter. Those fourth and tenth traditions apparently, in legal terms, make this clear. Surely, given the pretense of lawyers to sue the socks off anything, God is watching over us.

But as we warn. This too may pass. We are only one judgment away from the rug being pulled out from under us. Thus, we are *all* responsible to anyone anywhere who reaches out to ensure the hand of AA is always there. I say this as if our lives depend on it because it does. Thirteen stepping cannot be brushed under the rug to hide its occurrences. When we say, sunlight is the best disinfected, we should mean it.

Sexual assault is illegal. Many in Midtown have come forward. Appropriate action by the proper authorities took place. Unfortunately, breach of trust and manipulation is not criminal. It's immoral and unethical for sure, but not illegal.

AA meetings, (not the program) are mostly unregulated and loosely organized. The scoundrels that are here today, are just as likely to be gone tomorrow. Still, be careful of any meeting that's described as a barroom without the booze, or a meat market where all the cuts are cheap.

Thankfully, "they're all in on it" cult-like thirteenth stepping groups are rare. They are only made possible when there is a lack of God's presence in all our affairs. We only have a daily reprieve, be it with the individual, or the group. The tell-tale warning signs that a meeting is more cult, and less AA include:

- A defined and structured group leadership.
- A sponsee was "assigned" their sponsor.
- A "buck in the basket" is never enough.
- Group members were only "allowed" to attend Midtown-affiliated meetings.
- Newcomers were prohibited from discussing group business with outsiders.
- Taking any prescribed medicine was just "chewing your booze".
- In need of a place to stay? Rent only from one of the group's approved landlords.
- Needed something from the store? You better get it at "Mr. Q's". He's one of us.
- Young women sleeping with old men, well that's in the book (?). We're not the sex police.
- Turning sixteen is the go ahead to, "Get'em before God does."

In conjunction with the Newsweek story, the damage done by Midtown was contained. And while AA GSO had no comment on that matter, it hasn't remained silent. AA published a Safety Card. It clearly says anonymity is not a cloak for covering up unethical, disruptive, and illegal actions. You can get called out in, and kicked out of, a meeting. Wrongdoers cannot hide in AA. There is no attorney/client, or doctor/patient relationship protections. AA makes no claim that there is. This, the courts have decided too.

The best way to protect yourself is by protecting others. If you keep one eye looking left, they can keep one scanning right. And in spotting a stepper assume the role of Paul Revere. *"The steppers are coming! The Steppers are coming!*

Being cognizant of the danger doesn't mean walking around in fear. Make no mistake about it, a stepper fears exposure as the vampire fears the cross. They can't ply their trade if their reputation shrivels into the rot, it is. Unfortunately, any relief is fleeting and soon lost. For they can, and will, move on to a new meeting. Don't chase them. It's not your job. And if you keep up the chase, it will become resentment. Think about how humiliated you'll be making amends for this. You'll be giving the stepper exactly what they want. Which is power over you.

The privilege of being autonomous and anonymous comes from our Traditions. They are anchored in trust. However, for any fast-thinking, double-dealing, shit-stirring, cross-talking, thirteenth-stepping conniver, interpretation is in the beholder's eye. Let's look at our traditions from a 13th-step point of view.

1. My welfare first, all others second. For the stepper, it's all about them. Enough said.
2. There are no AA police. When the cat's away, the rats will play.
3. We refuse no one. To each their own, and I want that one.
4. Each group is governed by its own conscience. A stepper has no God-consciousness.
5. Our primary purpose is to carry our message. You have your way. The stepper has theirs.
6. Money, property, and power divert our spiritual aim. The main weapon of the thirteenth stepper is their charisma. We go along to get along.
7. Each group is self-supporting. If it sounds too good to be true, it probably isn't. There is no free lunch and all sex comes with a price.
8. We are non-professional. This make's the vulnerable easy pick'ens for the stepper willing to give "it" away for free.
9. We are an unorganized organization. Execution of a service position is supposed to be fiduciary and custodial. The stepper will publicly declare, "AA's an honest program", (wink, wink, nudge, nudge). When heard, remember these words, "the more they proclaimed their honesty, the faster we counted the spoons."
10. We have no opinion on outside issues. What goes on in the parking lot, stays in the parking lot.
11. Personal anonymity is the cloak that hides. Being anonymous has but one purpose. To deceive.
12. We place principles before personalities. If asked, "Do you want to see my Big Book?" Take heed—caveat emptor.

Soldiers stay off well-traveled trails because they're booby-trapped. If you go into a private chat barroom in Zoom, you'll be grabbed. Alcoholism is not a random act. Peace of mind will not come from being click-baited, memed, or blog-smeared. The moment a malicious miscreant gets your internet fix, you'll be infected.

A word about Zoom®. A thirteen-stepping brute has no boundaries. Being in a box, you may think you're staring on Hollywood Square's but to the stepper you're in a cell. They're looking at your surroundings for clues. "Is that your cat", they ask in chat. When on Zoom, dress as you would at a live meeting. If you don't want unwanted attention drawn to you fit in, not stand out. Attention is a powerful drug. One that requires more and more once you get a taste for it. Beware of wanting to be the most important person in the room.

Don't get me wrong. Zoom meetings are great. In fact, the Big Book Forward to Fourth Edition (2001) predicted modem-to-modem meetings. That's right up there with the 1939 man on the moon one. All I'm saying is be extra careful not to get yourself ambushed by a bunch of electrons.

And if you find yourself in the crosshairs of a stepping sniper maneuvering in for a "back rub hug" ambush? Move away quickly, find cover, and tell Miss Jane. Don't shoot back. You may hit an innocent target. And that would really suck. And if you move too late? Go stiff and don't hug back. If you don't give them what they need they will suspect you're a booby trap. Combat requires muscle memory, instinctual reactions, and knowing when to fire and when to maneuver. If you act like you know how to defend yourself, they most likely won't come back for more. As we paratroopers say, the best way to get out of a minefield is don't jump into one.

If push comes to shove there is a legal remedy. A restraining order, while drastic, if needed is there. There are lawyers in the program from which one can seek advice. Don't be too quick on the draw with this. You may shoot yourself in the foot and another drunk in the back. It should only be used when unwanted attention is outside the confines of the fellowship. For example, if you're being harassed, stalked, or threatened with violence.

So, how does one recognize a stepper? Keep it simple. What we do speaks louder than anything we say. There may come a time when the lamb will lay down with the lion. But until that actually happens, always put your money on the lion. Doveryay, No Proveryay,

Having love and losing it is part of life. So is not having love and wanting it. In either case, you don't feel good about yourself. Live and learn gets no competition from love'em and leave 'em. And while a moving target is hard to hit, the one that escapes has a tale to tell. Passing on what you know about the 13th step is best left to those who are uniquely qualified to do so.

Gabrielle Glaser is a journalist. In her 2013 book, *Her Best-Kept Secret: Why Women Drink—And How They Can Regain Control,* she acknowledges AA saves lives. She also categorically states, "AA is particularly a wrong choice for women." Why? Because it's 13th Step based.

To make this point, Glaser, who is not an alcoholic, "scoured" AA's Big Book for clues to crack its misogynist code. Finding He and Him to reference God was prima facie evidence beyond any reasonable doubt that AA was a misogynistic, monopolistic, non-scientific cult of maniacal male personalities. A clique of deplorable infidels. One with a stranglehold around the waist of all women, as evident by "that AA type" of a hug.

Glaser's view on "thirteen stepping" has merit. Like any million-person organization, AA has a fractional minority of the unsavory who prey on their fellows. They can be a newcomer or have many twenty-four hours. They are not always male and not always straight. They are constantly on the prowl. However, our "primary purpose" doesn't allow kicking them out of AA. Let me say in response to Ms. Glaser, that one grain of sand doesn't represent the whole beach.

AAs fellowship component is half of the whole. Without it, we'd just read the book. And all things being equal, after the first couple of pages we'd need a drink in hand just to flip the page. That's why sober dances and cookouts are so important. They take us away from ourselves so we don't have to be with ourselves. After all, being alone got us here.

Recovering twenty-four seven, three sixty-five is hard for us to think about. We have things to do, places to go, and a life to live. We have a lot to think about. The mind is like a slot machine. It spins all day long. When off the beam, our thoughts often land on, "I suck." Why? Because we are at the controls and pulling the handle. We say we trust and rely on God, but are quick to say, "I'll take it from here."

We can't stay in a church basement or in a Zoom room all day. There are periods of action and inaction in the fellowship when you're out on your own. In living life on life terms, going with the flow sometimes requires rowing upstream. And since God doesn't row when we want to steer, it's assured we'll be going in circles.

Alcoholism is an equal opportunity destroyer. With the use and abuse of mind-altering substances, "privilege" offers zero protection. AA is not an equal opportunity restorer. We have no monopoly on what works and what doesn't. We only have a way that works for some of us. Who gets in your lifeboat? You can't control it; it's the chance we take. That bag lady smoking like she's in front of a firing squad could be a saint. While that guy everybody thinks is really deep may be a clandestine purveyor of debauchery and exploitation. This makes AA a veritable melting pot. Hang together or hang separately.

As of 2022, AA is in 180 countries, with 2.1 million members attending 160,000 meetings. The Center for Disease Control estimates 4½ percent of the US male population and 2½ of the female meet the DSM-V definition of alcohol abuse. Based on the 2020 census of 325 million, this equals the potential for 11.6 million alcoholics. We better order some more paper cups.

The *American Psychiatric Association Diagnostic and Statistical Manual, Fifth Edition (DSM-V),* categorizes alcoholism as a Substance Abuse Dependence Disorder. Its acronym is SADD. How appropriate.

Some of us are sadder than others. Once free of drugs and alcohol, we seek relief in food, gambling, shopping, money, power, and sex. Writing it all down and letting it go didn't relieve all the pain. This book won't help with that.

We bring into AA what brought us there. Just not drinking is not the cure for alcoholism. In fact, just not drinking can make some of those worst items in stock come to life. The problem with drugs and alcohol is they work. And when not in our system, we need to seek a make me feel good substitute. And when at an AA meeting, what's the closest thing at hand? That's right, another drunk. Preferably one that's hoping to find an easier, softer way. For the stepper, this is like shooting fish in a barrel.

Making love is a euphemism for sex. Going out is one for drinking. What do Rudolph and Bill W. have in common? Both are the most famous of all. One as a reindeer, the other as a thirteenth stepper. Yes, it's a poor joke, but it's also true. We are not accountable for the sins of the father. Only that we pass on our traditions from one AA generation to the next. We make no excuses for the human failings of our members; no matter who they are. Unfortunately, this concept sounds better in words than in practice.

The successful stepper knows how to talk the talk without walking the walk. Instead, they slither along hiding, bobbing, and weaving. The stepper's principal weapon is not seduction, it's stealth. Evade, cover, conceal and escape. Their offensive power is charisma. They appear charming, interesting, and caring. They're often spontaneous, intense, funny, and sexy. They have their groupies.

This makes it tricky to identify them. If approached and interrogated, they turn the tables claiming victim, not victimizer. It's all a ruse. Like a spider on a web, they make the environment they inhabit look inviting and safe when it's not.

Stepper's sham emotion. They're the big man on campus one day and the bottom of the pile the next. Self-victimization is just another weapon in their arsenal. They know the art of self-pity only works when there is a sympathetic audience at hand. It's not surprising such versatility easily seduces others. They live to dominate the doormat. They get their thrills out of wiping their feet on other people.

Attention, affection, attraction, and aggrandizement fill holes we all have within our psychics. Everybody wants to be wanted. Nobody wants a dented can. Except for the thirteenth stepper. They'll take anything they can get. They'll just throw it away when they've had enough of it.

However, the stepper's power is not infinite. In fact, it's quite limited. It solely depends on the cooperation of the victim. You'd think having a passing awareness of the threat, the victims would be few. You'd be wrong. For if being up to your neck in quicksand doesn't bother you, then why would you want to be pulled out?

The stepper intentionally misinterprets signals. Especially if in the negative tense. It's not that they can't take no for an answer; it's they won't. Espionage is more than snaking and sneaking around, it's disinformation too. We say be careful of the lies we tell ourselves. This is because they are the hardest to disprove. Conversely, it is also true we must be careful of the lies told to us by others. The artful steppers know how to hold out a branch of hope to the hopeless.

Let's look at the modus operandi of the stepper. Here their tools of the trade:

- Offer of a ride to/from the meeting
- Showing up uninvited at unusual times or places
- Stories that solicit sympathy, empathy, compassion, understanding, and love
- They wallow in self-pity, giving thanks that at least you "understand"
- Demands of "Do that this way."
- They spell praying as preying.
- They use social media or technology as a means to keep track of you.

And the harm done:

- It's detrimental to a group's stability
- They can ruin the reputation of the fellowship
- The collateral damage done deters others from seeking our help
- Disloyalty and deceit desecrate trust
- Foster feelings of fear, shame, guilt, and remorse.
- They jeopardize sobriety. Not theirs, yours.

An ambush only works when there is cover and concealment. Before being found out, the stepper needs to get in and out. The perfect ambush goes: stalk them, grab them, ghost them, forget them, then move on to another. The perfect escape leaves the victim wondering, "What did I do?" It's all so predictable.

Artillery is predictably unpredictable. It's like Bingo. Everywhere rounds drop, hoping for a hit. This means artillery causes much collateral damage. Missing the target with the first round is never a deterrence. The stepper is constantly dropping rounds and adjusting fire. If you're praying for someone to make you happy, you're praying to be preyed on.

When someone gets stepped on, who gets chased out? The perp or the victim? It depends. If it's the "let it go laureates" stepper enablers that make the call. Then it's not even close. These go-along-to-get-along types are wannabe masters of love and tolerance. They think either there's nothing that can be done, or we (interpreted as men) are all like that. How wrong they are on both counts.

To be fair, women manipulate men as well. David had a one-night stand, and Vincent cut off his ear. And Micky? He had a pickup truck. So, as the sole proprietor of the Might Get Lucky Moving Company, Micky did a lot of *pro bono* moving. All he wanted was a chance. Being the first-born son of an Irish mother, Micky came into this world angry, horny, and needing a drink. And since the 13th step is not always sexual, Micky proved, again and again, that no good deed goes unpunished. Still, he had a lot of fun being taken advantage of. As *Life* goes, "Give it to Micky. He'll take anything."

Manipulation and deception are the stepper's tools of the trade. That's why the prep gets a pass. After all, they have time in service, time in grade. The Roman Numerals on their medallions validate this. They use "I've been around long enough" to gain AA superiority. It's also efficient for sob stories, sympathy, and self-pity. They don't become group-stepper-in-chief without setting up a sham facade.

On the opposite end of the debate is the "we know better than you crowd." These are the ones who love rules. Thanks to them, the meeting opening and secretary report take up 2/3 of the time. Okay, that's an exaggeration. But you know who I mean. They call an emergency group conscience because there was no cream for the coffee. With them, it's doing as I say, not what I do. And what do they do? In acknowledging the 13th step; nothing.

These types want AA to enjoy a reputation they know in their heart it doesn't deserve. It's like, God forbid, our drinking buddies find out we go to AA. They will never believe that a thirteenth stepper belongs to "*their*" meeting. Those *guys* only go to those *other* groups. The ones *we* would never go to. They can't understand that in the land of the blind, the one-eyed man is king.

And who we see, and what we say, should stay inside our halls. This includes business meetings. Never make the stepper the focus. Targeted accusations, innuendo, and suggestions of inappropriate individual behaviors sounds like sour grapes. And a wine made from sour grapes doesn't age well at all. A generalized discussion of what is not acceptable should be the fruits of this harvest. Inclusion of a warning and availability of AA's "safety card" in the secretary's report may deter the active and potential thirteenth stepper from crossing that line.

All of us who come to the fellowship lead a double life. We know a damaged reputation when we see one. Which means we also know how to hide. Only after being absolutely, positively, and totally defeated do we concede our four basic fears.

- Fear of other people's opinions.
- Fear of losing what we have.
- Fear of not getting what we want.
- Fear of being found out.

Thirteenth steppers rarely mention having God in their lives. They know if they open that door, God will stand there with a restraining order. They intuitively know if they were really "working" the program, they wouldn't be working on you. If you are next on their list, it's your fault. You've taken the 14th step. You let them get away with it because they can.

Back in the beginning, I described the 13th step as a violation of trust. Sobriety isn't easy. We must sweep away several lifelong conceptions. And one of the hardest to sweep away is the one we need someone on the arm to make us feel good about ourselves. Why is this? It's because we trust in the finite self rather than trusting in an infinite God.

Addicts know all about trust. Didn't we meet some stranger behind Walmart and hand them a hundred for a baggie of something? How is falling for the thirteenth stepper's best "come on" lines any different? We are used to being taken advantage of. What difference does sobriety make when you come to expect just more of the same? Predators, like dealers, know this to be true. That's why they know all about how to get you to do what you don't want to do.

So, if tempted, fall back, speak up, and don't go back for more. Seek the 1SG. He'll remind you of the Army's four what-to-do of the Be, Know, Do doctrine of defense. Fortify your position. Set up obstacles. Establish a kill zone. Watch those boundaries.

A major misconception is the offenders are protected. That AA's anonymity, its disorganized organization, and group autonomy tradition, protect against wrongdoing. It doesn't. What protects the thirteenth stepper is apathy and charisma. We go along, so they can get along.

This allows the group's favorite-son offender to hide in plain sight. How ironic it is that the offended gets chased away. Yet, the offender wallows in the adulation of speaking truth to power. Not a Higher Power, but their power. The most dangerous stepper of all is the one everybody likes. They are often popular speakers. They make us laugh on Monday. Cry on Tuesday. And feel sorry for them every day of the week. To go along to get along, everyone looks the other way. They believe they have earned the right to deceive. After all, nobody calls them out. Instead, it's a don't rock the boat, don't make us look bad, this too shall pass. But it won't. It's one thing to know the lexicon of AA, and quite another to know what to do.

Here are some signs you're a target of the 13th Step in progress:

- Going to a bar or engaging in other risky behaviors.
- Reminiscing about the good times when drinking and drugging.
- Inviting themselves over to your place. You letting them in.
- Getting intimate on the first date.
- Providing confidential info like how much you have in the bank.
- Any form of exploitative, intimidating, or engineered demands on your time.
- They or you have an unhappy home life.
- They or you have a history of affairs and/or successive short-term failed relationships.
- They or you have a heritable disorder or a family history of out-of-bounds conduct.
- They or you like to play "secret agent man."
- They or you have an is an excitement junkie.

All in AA are trusted servants. This means we have a duty to each other and the fellowship. This gives us no authority, only a purpose. And if we bring an allegation. Ms. Jane or the 1SG should speak to the alleged stepper in private. We should make no public accusation. We're not prosecutors, judges, juries, or executioners. Neither are we saints. Reminding them, that an ounce of prevention is worth more than a pound of cure, should make the point.

And if a private discussion yields no fruit? A group conscience could address the matter, without accusation, of the issue. This is an appropriate use of the cloak of anonymity. Here, the group may vote to amend their format to announce the availability of AA's Safety Card. The secretary report should reiterate, that if anyone disrupts the group, they'll be told to leave the meeting. That AA is not a place for unsafe or illegal behavior. And that such behavior will be reported to authorities. This does not go against AA's traditions. We must ensure the safety of all in attendance.

And if that doesn't work? Then smoke the stepper out. How? Make sex the discussion topic. They'll scram for the door. It's a tactic that works especially well when they know, you know, who they are.

AALIT

Is there really that much difference between, "Can I buy you a drink?" and "Would you like to go for coffee?" No, there isn't. Why? The asker doesn't want to hear no for an answer.

Want to know what makes a drunk happy? It's when they know others know they are right. That's why, when we don't get what we want, or people don't do what we tell them, we declare unequivocally, and without fear of contradiction; people suck! And the worst thing anyone can do when a drunk is in such a state is to say, "Okay, maybe you're right." Why is this? Because they will let no one forget it. The best we can hope for is that this too shall pass. But it won't.

Ted Bundy answered calls on a suicide prevention hotline. John Wayne Gacy was a clown. A suite of antisocial behavioral patterns characterizes psychopaths. These include lying, cheating, and stealing. These people live to exploit others for gain, pleasure, and power. Being unsympathetic and seductive, they ply their sadistic trade. They only care about themselves and show no remorse. There's little hope of them changing their ways because they see nothing wrong.

Harvard psychologist Martha Stout's book *The Sociopath Next Door* is an excellent read. In its pages, she tells you just what you don't want to hear. One in every twenty-five people you meet could be a sociopath in training. They are everywhere. One could be your ex-partner, your boss, your priest, professor, or fellow alcoholic. To make matters worse, you don't know what to look for. This is further complicated by when a sociopath is in training, they act like normal people most of the time. And when they don't, and consequences arise, they don't change but learn from their mistakes. It takes time, practice and determination to mature into a successful sociopathic stepper. And since a thirteen stepper has no conscience, they experience no shame, guilt, and remorse. For them, a remorseful mumbling, "I'm sorry", fits the bill. But what they are sorry for is being caught. They feel they can do anything they want because they feel no guilt.

On any day, 2.3 million individuals are incarcerated in the United States. That's AA's worldwide membership,. The cost is $260 billion annually. Many end up in the slammer, short and long term, because of the cause-and-effect of substance use. If there is a war on drugs and alcohol, we're losing. There must be a better way.

In 1980, a Florida county judge and prosecutor came up with the idea of a drug court. These judicial proceedings centered on diversionary programs. "What's your choice, Mr. Druggie or Ms. Alkie, treatment or jail?" The idea of second chance courts spread rapidly with promising results. By the mid ninetics, AA was being flooded with court-ordered attendees. Most didn't want to be there.

It's a myth that thirteenth stepping works on newly sober young and attractive women. No seasoned stepper thinks this way. Only the inexperienced wannabe stepping badass does. And their record is one of striking out every time at bat. If you're young and attractive, a stepper has no chance, so why bother? No, it's the needy and desperate they go after. These types offer a much higher ROI (return on investment) and the risk/reward ratio runs positive.

From rehab romance to meeting stakeouts, these types are on a search and destroy mission. Their tactics are rarely a frontal assault. Think about this. You're an old to middle-aged man, on the portly side, poorly educated, broke, and missing all your bottom teeth. Yeah, that twenty-something hottie will go ga-ga over you because you said, "Nice to hear ya." Could it happen? Sure, but how often? Never!

Not every thirteenth stepper goes to AA. But they go where the hunting might pay off. Going clubbing and dancing should be a good time. But dancing to the light fandango doesn't mean you can let your guard down. Roofies (Rohypnol ®) in a non-alcoholic drink are not unheard of. Drugged and dragged about, you're at their mercy. And with these types, mercy is in short supply.

When out and about, don't turn your back on what you're slugging. When on the dance floor, have a dedicated drink custodian. Watch your drink like it's your purse. And when walking about on the streets, keep your head on a swivel and a thumb on speed dial 9-1-1. And always let someone know where you're going, who you'll be with, and when you'll be home. Yes, I know this sounds like overshadowing chaperoning, but in this game, you only get one strike, then you're out.

From time to time, a stepper gets steps on. And when they do, they can't wait to bitch about it loud and clear. It's a ploy to get the sympathy vote. It's their yin pulling on our yang. This ancient philosophical concept dictates we are all interwoven together. Yet with the stepper, what comes around and goes around is, the vulnerable. Nothing can offset the damage they do.

We're told to live one day at a time, love and tolerance of others must be our code. However, while the goal is to be a Good Samaritan every day, we often discover no good deed goes unpunished.

LS-squared (LS)2 is an *alcohonym* that stands for Life Sucks Less Sober. This *alcohonyism* is brief, clear, and simple. It's the formula for understanding what we mean when we say, God can do for us, what we can't do for ourselves. Like when we are told, "Just say no." But when does no, not mean no? It's when no, actually means maybe. And since maybe, is not a no, then it must be a yes. This is an axiom.

An axiom defeats an argument by insisting a point of view is a fact. It has nothing to do with the truth. For example, you can't prove to an alcoholic they have a drinking problem because an alcoholic has no problem with drinking. Alcoholics won't do what they are told to do and always do what they're told not to do. We codify logic of this sort as an AALIT or Alcoholic Axiomatic Laws of Illogical Thinking.

AALIT I: This first alcoholic law is the Non-Contradiction Contradiction or, "It is what it is." This annoying phrase is the basis of all alcoholic axiomatic logic. To test this, go out drinking at the Come Again Lounge. Pound down anything a stranger puts in front of you. Make sure to nod your head every time anyone says, "She'll have another." When the last call sounds, order a "double" one for the road. Do this, and you'll understand the underpinnings of the axiomatic law that, yes, everybody does look good at closing time. It also explains why there is a car in the parking lot come morning. "It is what it is, and that's that."

AALIT II: This is the Law of the Excluded Unexcluded. For the alcoholic, there is no middle of the road. We're right, you're wrong. Like AALIT I, this second AALIT is an undisputed deduction of an alcoholic's illusion and delusion. Any unacceptable corollary to the contrary is unreliably undeniably unbelievably undesirable, provided it's unequivocally due to its unamiability. Or, to sum it up, what makes an alcoholic happy is when you know they are right.

AALIT III: The Unidentifiable Identity Law is like the first two laws, except that it isn't. In alcoholic thinking, the alcoholic discovers the truth by denying the obvious. That makes it possible for the alcoholic who is unarmed with the facts about themselves to deny any of it is factual. With this law, it's not that you're either an alcoholic or you're not, but whether you can get away with it.

The fourth Alcoholic Axiomatic Law of Illogical Thinking brings the three earlier AALIT Laws together. It's brief, clear, and simple—people suck. You know this is true because it doesn't apply to you. As an alcoholic with an alcoholic mind, our troubles are the making of others. Thus, we can cancel out our own suckness, proving everybody is wrong about everything, and the world and its people are out to get us. This brings us right back to the reason we drink in the first place: we want to be left alone and do what we want.

Masquerading as an anti-reality is where making the wrong choice is the obvious choice. And what is it we choose to believe? It's always someone else's fault. Why? Because we're positive people suck. And how do we know everybody else sucks? They don't do what we want. And the reason they don't do what we want is that they suck. Now, who can argue with that?

Let's review. For alcoholics, there is but one axiom that matters. It's the indisputable, unrefuted, uninterrupted, absolute truth that states categorically and without fear of contradiction that what makes an alcoholic happy is when you know they are right. Don't forget that.

Et Tu, Brute?

A searching and fearless moral inventory from time to time does no harm. In fact, it helps to clear away any wreckage from the past that washes up on shore.

While statistics to prove this point are unavailable. Personal observation tells me criminal rape and assault in AA are rare. I say this because rape and assault, it's one and done. You can't keep something like that secret.

It's also my opinion, on the whole, that sexual harassment from snowflake to flamethrower is below par. I say this because with harassment we all know it when we see it, and boy, do we hear about it when it happens. To measure proportionality, I submit with proclaiming victimhood, we in AA have no seconds. Maybe I'm naïve, or just deaf, dumb, and blind. However, I just don't see it. What I see is how a 13th step creeps work.

We see from our fourth step that in wanting to be wanted, we cannot be picky. It isn't the right kind if we don't get enough. We pass no judgment on what you wrote. We're not the arbitrator of anyone's sex conduct. All of us have sex problems. This means there is no such thing as a "controlled" addiction. If you think yours is, it's one of those lies we tell ourselves.

Collateral alcoholic trauma is not always dynamic. It builds incrementally. Sociologists say unacceptable behavior fixates early. Emotional isolation is often a warning sign. Although this is not true for everyone, the first trauma is as traumatizing as the last. These give rise to the thought that many of today's perpetrators were yesterday's victims. Their trauma is symbiotic and parasitic.

Revenge for harm perceived is a powerful driving force. It bestows a sense of justice. And the truth may be, today's perpetrators were yesterday's victims. This is a reason, not an excuse. Using sex and its accouterments is no antidote for pain. Instead, it's the cause. Not for them, but for others. Remember, selfishness and self-centeredness is the root of *all* our troubles. Having power over others is not just a drug. It's the prescription they write for themselves. One that comes solely at a cost to others.

Experiences underlie the abuse of drugs, alcohol, and people. A desire to harm others means there is something wrong somewhere. We mishandle drugs and alcohol because that is part of the disorder. Yes, I said disorder. Why? Because DSM-V says psychopathic, sociopathic, and borderline personality disorders are a malfunction in the mind. And we suffer from a hopeless condition of mind and body. We can recover from but never cured. Thankfully, these types are few among us. They can't stand to hear the truth. So, most of them don't hang around too long.

Trauma is not coincidental to sexual abuse; it's a guarantee. If abused, don't keep it a secret. With that said, it's debatable if an abuser belongs on your sex list. I think they belong to resentment or fear. Fear is the most probable. However, as always, when in doubt, go to God, talk it out, and do as you're told.

If you're a victim of rape, incest, abuse, or enslavement, someone in AA will identify with you. These are traumatizing criminal acts. AA is not the place for justice. We don't supply mental health, medical care, or investigative resources for crime, trauma, or PTSD issues. These are best left to those dedicated to doing so.

While relying on God is essential, one should not disregard human help. Outside therapy can play a pivotal role in recovery. One-on-one office visits are person-centered and private. Church basement hangouts, even when empathetic, humanistic, and authentic, may not provide what you need. It's truly impressive how much a professional can do for us when they don't come with the baggage we do. Even if we go only to hand the therapist the $15 co-pay, and ask them how they're doing, much good comes from sharing your plans, dreams, and schemes with them.

Honesty is the antithesis of selfishness. These two just cannot get along. Trying to mix them together causes huge emotional and mental disruptions. That's why when acting out on an old behavior; it's not an old behavior. Instead, it's a guest star appearance of the old self. And unless contained at once, immediately and quickly, we're off and running the show again. Everyone can do things we said we would never do.

Skeletons, we hope, will never see the light of day. But they are buried in shallow graves. Being angry, indignant, and oozing self-pity only stops when we come to believe God will do for us what we cannot do for ourselves. This is the basis of we used to think one way, and now we think another. Only then will we know the freedom of bondage of self. No longer does the world and its people dominate us.

We must grow toward our future sexual ideal and make amends for past indiscretions. Going forward, we'll invite God in before proceeding. We'll ask for the strength and sanity to do the right thing. If we ask God what to do? The right answer will come.

Engaging in thirteenth step behavior is wrong. We pay a price. But this doesn't mean a death sentence. You can give yourself a break. Every thirteenth step story has at least two sides to it. This doesn't mean there is equity. The truth of who did what to whom will remain between them. But the absolute truth is a drunk can never drink in safety. And if you are afraid of what's behind you, you'll never feel safe.

Self-forgiveness is not a contradiction. It's a second chance at another second chance. In AA, you can have as many second chances as you need. You need not explain. We too have been where you are at. We understand as no others do.

How do we pay back this debt? There are innumerable ways to make reparations. You can take that GSR job nobody wants and do it well. Double up on the buck in the basket. Work with that one drunk you just can't stand. You'll soon find out they are just like you. Show up early, stay late, unlock the door, turn on the lights, make the coffee, and clean up after.

When something works, we keep it up. When it doesn't? We try to wrest or take by force, what we want. We demand to be happy, joyous, and free, no matter who we hurt to get there. Drunks come into AA as liars, cheats, and thieves. And until there is an essential psychic change, a vital spiritual experience, and new moral psychology, we are still liars, cheats, and thieves. This is until we accept those three pertinent ideas: I can't, you can't, but He could.

Addiction is a sickness. If you're stepping out, step on another, eventually you're going to get stepped on too.

One of the hardest truths to swallow is claiming to be a victim does not make you one. A victim is not responsible for what befalls them. A victim cannot choose to walk away. A threat of force takes that freedom away. A victim has no power to say no. And yes, you said no. But then you changed your mind. Why? Because we want what we want when we want it. This, a stepper knows. It's what they count on.

When one's spiritual defenses are weak, no doesn't mean no. It means maybe. And since maybe is not a no, then it must mean yes. When no means no, make sure you spell it right. This shouldn't be that hard since no is the first word we learn. And until handed that first drink and asked, "Do you want one?" it's all we knew what to say.

It's with this first yes, we are off to the drug and alcohol races. Though we come out of the gate fast, we are soon round the bend. And before we know it, we can't make it to the end. Sex with someone who's so under the influence or was "worked on" brings no satisfaction. Only a desire for more. It's a need that can never be met. Why is this? Because while you may be "all in", there's nothing in return. Regardless of which side of the coin you fall, if you go back for more, you're not a victim, but a volunteer. If someone wants to read the sex part of their fourth step, to you – say ooh-yuck and run away. Don't pass go. Don't collect the $200. Just go.

47

Hubris and humiliation yield shame, guilt, and remorse. And shame, guilt, and remorse work best when we suffer in silence. When we are alone with unpleasant thoughts, we seek relief by taking a drink. And for us, to drink is to die. Many fumbles the ball on the first play. Not coming back after being stepped on is letting them kick you when you're down. Humility doesn't come from being a doormat. It comes from showing up after the humiliation.

What's important in making amends is knowing the part you play. It's not about blame or shame, but change. The idea of amends is to prevent a reoccurrence of those behaviors that cause us to say "I'm sorry" in the first place. Guilt comes from what you did, and shame comes from how you feel about what you did. This is the flaw in trying to deal with a stepper. They do not see what they did as wrong.

Some signs to watch for in a stepper include:

They have an addictive personality. They excluded nothing. Drugs, alcohol, money, power, sex, food, whatever. If you have it, they want it. If they already have enough, they want more. Their appetite is ravenous. What's not given, they take.

Air of superiority. Have a question? They have the answer. You did it this way. Well, that was wrong. These types don't have to prove to the world they are important, because they know they are.

Alienation of their private life from AA. They want to know everything about you while telling you nothing about themselves. Any inquiries of who they are, what they do, or where they come from are met with aversion, rudeness, or even hostility.

Cavalier and charismatic. This is the most common trait. They can't get away with it if nobody likes to be around them.

Audacious and intense impulsivity. It's the rush of the chase that gives them "the high."

Vulnerable to self-esteem, doubt, or insecurity. There can be no critique or criticism of who or what they are. Their ego is expansive. Like malignant cancer. Its cystidium spreads through every thought, word, deed, and action. Thee who dare cross will feel their wrath.

Over sensitive and underwhelming. They can dish it out, but not take it.

Intrigued by the next new thing. This "shiny object syndrome" is not unique to this classification of people. Most of us have a touch of ADHD and a dusting of OCD too. Our attention to detail, when in danger, is often derailed by petty thoughts of regretting the past and dreading the future.

They are "counters". Gunslingers would put notches on their guns to keep score. They take no prisoners and they do shoot the wounded. Keeping score is the way they tell themselves, "See, I'm better than you."

Suppose we fall short. Maybe we put a toe into the waters of a 13th step and even liked it. Maybe we want more. Having made a good beginning, we fall back, regroup, and replenish our spiritual ammo. Here, we converse with God and examine our motives. If we are sorry, willing to set matters straight, and learned a lesson, all is forgiven. But if the conduct continues, we will drink. This is a great fact for us. Only the sickest of the sick can go on unaffected.

One platitude of the program is of being a power of example. But what's more enlightening are poor examples. For what we do speaks louder than anything we say. This brings to mind the thirteenth stepper's mantra, "Do as I say, not as I do." With this in mind, take this yes or no, 13th step quiz.

- Do you see meetings as a barroom without the booze? In scanning the room, do you think, "I'd do that one, and that one, and that one too?"
- Need to move? Flirt with Micky because he has a pickup truck.
- Asking someone you just met saying, "I know a great meeting. When can I pick you up?"
- Your sexual ideal is, "Get'em before God does," meaning (a) before they die; (b) after they drink; or (c) before they take the second step.
- Told the newcomer, who only introduced themselves, "Nice to hear ya."
- Being a magnet for the vicissitude-inclined trauma-drama queens? Believing the sicker, the better.
- Steal vicarious pleasures by asking, "Do you want to go to a 'whoopee' party with me?"
- Do you dress to impress?
- In helping others, was a personal gain to be had? Is it hard to differentiate between a den of ill-repute and the "sober house" you own?
- Getting someone to sleep with you is "God's will."
- Sponsoring the one you might get lucky with.
- In case you need anything, here's my number. And by the way, what's your address? Does anybody live with you?
- I heard your sink backed up. I'm a handyman, wink, wink, nudge, nudge.
- Wanna see my Big Book? I'd love to teach you, *How It Works*.
- Approach a "crier" and hug them again, and again, and again. Don't forget the associated check for bra back rub.
- Yes, I'm married. But that was a long time ago, and she doesn't understand me now.
- Have you offered one of us who is between addresses, a bed at your house?
- You speak of spirituality, sobriety, sanity, and serenity (SX4), hoping to score.
- You hate coffee, but ask anyone and everyone, "Wanna go for coffee?"

Of course, this quiz is my Irish mischief at play. We're in the world to play the role God assigns. I got wise ass. I only want to point out that a flirtatious smile does not make you guilty of a 13th step in the first degree. And if you have a violation on your record, don't be too hard on yourself. There's an infinite distance between this and that. Your only need from now on is to ask God, what is it you want me to be? Relationships, drunk or sober, are a lot easier to get into than get out of.

Not everyone agrees with my observations. AA has many critics. Many bear witness to an AA experience that is nothing more than a barroom without the booze. I think they're wrong. But here's some precautionary advice.

Keep a safe distance. This includes physically, emotionally, and electronically. If you don't trust them, stay away from them. It's better to be safe than sorry. And, if in time your "gut feeling" proves to be in error, then you can make a new beginning. Amends are not needed. We make amends for what we did, not what we think.

Don't disseminate personal information from the podium. It says our stories disclose in a *general way*. So, don't reveal specifics such as where you live, your income, or where you spend your quiet time. Tell those things only to those who have a valid need to know. If pestered by someone for your number, give them 9-1-1, this should scare them off. And speaking of 9-1-1, make sure it's on speed dial when out and about alone.

Group activities require three or more. Going on a speaking commitment with that Raffle Ticket Romeo is taking the bait. If you want to tell "your story" do so, but only if you bring a friend of your choosing. If nothing else, it will ruin the steppers' little plans and designs for this day.

No one else can "make it all better." We have our three pertinent ideas: "I can't, you can't, but God could." Follow these directions on the firing line of life, and God will keep you unharmed. And, when in the line of fire, keep your head down.

There's no need to be rude. Being courteous while firm is not easily mistaken as flirtatious. A polite decline, made loud enough to be heard by those in proximity, is a proper warning. "Thanks for inviting me, but I'm unavailable." A civil rebuff saves face, deters advances, and keeps you safe.

Take nothing for granted. No matter who they are, or how long you've known them if intimate involvement is likely, first things first. Google the bastard! Not after, but before. A few keystrokes are could make a big difference in the decision-making process. It's best to have your eyes open to see who is trying to please or deceive.

Make the first few incursions in public. Remember, the 13th step modus operandi is to get in and get out before being found out. Any time spent cultivating an improbable score is an "opportunity lost" on a sure thing. Perpetrators of the 13th step don't waste time and money to get what they want. And if they don't get what they want on the first try, there will probably be no second date. With this in mind, order the most expensive thing on the menu and insist they leave a huge tip.

If you abide by these measures, you'll no longer make a heavy going of life. With God as your navigator, you'll always be heading in the right direction. When I speak, I like to end with a passage out of *A Vision For You*. And, with a few editorial changes, it goes like this.

And thus we grow, and so can you. But you be but one person with this book in your hand, we believe, it's all you need to begin. To duplicate what we have accomplished is simply a matter of willingness, patience, and labor. May God keep you and protect you. All the way. Airborne!

Butterflies and Paratroopers Are Not Born With Wings

"You gotta buy it, It's a riot."

This is not a regurgitated recovery book. First, it's funny. Second, it's one-of-a-kind. And third, it's not a self-help book. It's an operator's manual. It trains alcoholics, drug addicts, overeaters, codependents, and whatever else has an addictive personality with a smidge of OCD or dusting of ADHD how to operate the most complex, prone to breakdown, out-of-warranty piece of equipment ever made—that's you.

In 1989, one in ten in recovery were women. Thirty-three years hence, it's one in three. Milo's sobriety date is April Fool's Day, 1989. He asked a woman out on a date, and some guy took him to an AA meeting. So, if you don't think God has a sense of humor, you'd be wrong.

Butterflies and Paratroopers is written from the perspective of a retired Army paratrooper and air traffic controller. The author 'was there' when women first entered these male only occupations. He knows a woman warrior when he sees one.

With an iron fist in a velvet glove, the persona of a First Sergeant trains a butterfly to be a paratrooper. *"We used to think one way, and now we think another."* Developing a new philosophy requires clarity of thought. And the clarity of thought comes from knowing who you are? Why you are like that? And why it's important to change?

Using amusing "girl-snippets", and "recovery war stories", Milo connects real-life trials and tribulations with spirituality, sobriety, sanity, and serenity. You'll quickly see the similarities between twelve-step recovery programs and the army. They take anybody and have a wrench to fit every nut that walks through the door.

Brevity, clarity, simplicity is the mantra. If you're talking about the problem, you can't be working on the solution. B&P is written so you can open it anywhere, start reading, and find solutions. With wit and cynicism, Milo reworks the army's doctrine of *BE, KNOW, DO: Train to Win in a Complex World* to describe a program of action, design for living, and process of recovery that seems to work with people like us. And who are people like us? We are the ones who have tried everything else.

If you are ready; the time is right. Put your jump boots on ladies, you're going to Jump School.

About the Author

Milo is a retired Army First Sergeant with more than thirty-three years of continuous sobriety. He received a Master's Degree in Public Administration from the University of New Hampshire and a Certificate of Graduate Studies from Harvard. A former paratrooper, air traffic controller, and auxiliary nuclear reactor operator, he was "in the room" when women first broke into these traditionally male roles. While serving in the army, he completed the Addiction Counselor Education Program at Boston University, and, besides being a First Sergeant, served as substance abuse and suicide prevention NCO. Now as a tired, old, bald, grumpy, and dumpy white guy, he shuffles between New Hampshire and Texas going to meetings with his Irish Setter, Madaline.

Made in the USA
Monee, IL
15 November 2022

17814224R00031